This book belongs to

I can get through this

When Parents Divorce or Separate

I Can Get Through This

By Lynn Cassella-Kapusinski

Pauline
BOOKS & MEDIA
Boston

Library of Congress Cataloging-in-Publication Data

Cassella-Kapusinski, Lynn.
 When parents divorce or separate : I can get through this / by Lynn Cassella-Kapusinski.
   p. cm. -- (A Catholic guide for kids)
 ISBN-13 978-0-8198-8342-1
 ISBN-10 0-8198-8342-5
 1. Divorce. 2. Children of divorced parents--Religious life. 3. Divorce--Religious
aspects--Christianity. I. Title.
 HQ814.C37 2012
  306.89--dc23   2012024519

The Scripture quotations contained herein are from the *New Revised Standard Version Bible: Catholic Edition,* copyright © 1989, 1993, Division of Christian Education of the National Council of the Churches of Christ in the United States of America. Used by permission. All rights reserved.

Scripture texts in this work are taken from the *New American Bible with Revised New Testament* and *Revised Psalms* © 1991, 1986, 1970 Confraternity of Christian Doctrine, Washington, D.C., and are used by permission of the copyright owner. All rights reserved. No part of the *New American Bible* may be reproduced in any form without permission in writing from the copyright owner.

Excerpts from the English translation of the *Catechism of the Catholic Church* for use in the United States of America, copyright © 1994, United States Catholic Conference, Inc. — Libreria Editrice Vaticana. Used with permission.

Cover and interior design by Mary Joseph Peterson, FSP

Chapter opening illustrations by Tabitha Perry; page 153 Brother Pharr; doodle contributions by Austin Wolfe, Maria Grace Dateno, FSP, Virginia Helen Richards, FSP, and Mary Joseph Peterson, FSP.

Published by Pauline Books & Media, 50 Saint Pauls Avenue, Boston, MA 02130-3491

Printed in the U.S.A.

WPDS VSAUSAPEOILL6-17J13-05503 8342-5

www.pauline.org

Pauline Books & Media is the publishing house of the Daughters of St. Paul, an international congregation of women religious serving the Church with the communications media.

The names in this book have been changed and the identities of the persons whose stories are told have been disguised in order to protect the confidentiality and sacredness of friendship and of the ministerial relationship.

1 2 3 4 5 6 7 8 9   16 15 14 13

This book is dedicated
with deep love and appreciation
to my wonderful husband,
George Kapusinski.
Without him and his immeasurable support
along this journey,
neither this book nor any of my ministry work
would have been possible.

Contents

A Note to the Reader

Dear Reader,

Hello! My name is Mrs. Kapusinski. A lot of young people call me "Mrs. K" for short. I'm so glad that you will be reading my book. It was given to you to help you learn and grow from your parents' separation, divorce, or remarriage. It can also help you if you have an absent parent, or if your parents never married and are now living apart.

You and I have something in common. My parents separated when I was eleven years old. That's why I wrote this book: because I know how tough this experience can be and how much it helps to get some guidance along the way. This book contains a lot of what I learned. I hope it makes your journey easier.

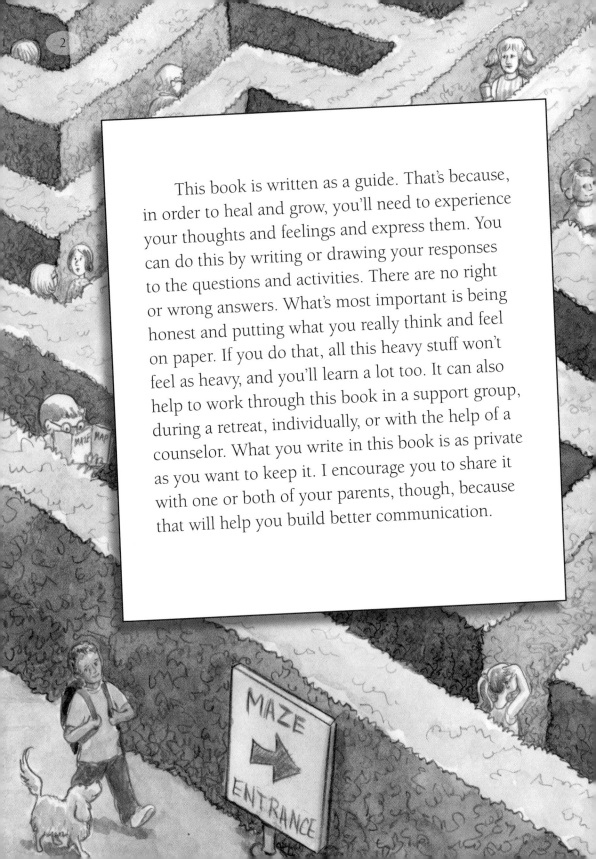

This book is written as a guide. That's because, in order to heal and grow, you'll need to experience your thoughts and feelings and express them. You can do this by writing or drawing your responses to the questions and activities. There are no right or wrong answers. What's most important is being honest and putting what you really think and feel on paper. If you do that, all this heavy stuff won't feel as heavy, and you'll learn a lot too. It can also help to work through this book in a support group, during a retreat, individually, or with the help of a counselor. What you write in this book is as private as you want to keep it. I encourage you to share it with one or both of your parents, though, because that will help you build better communication.

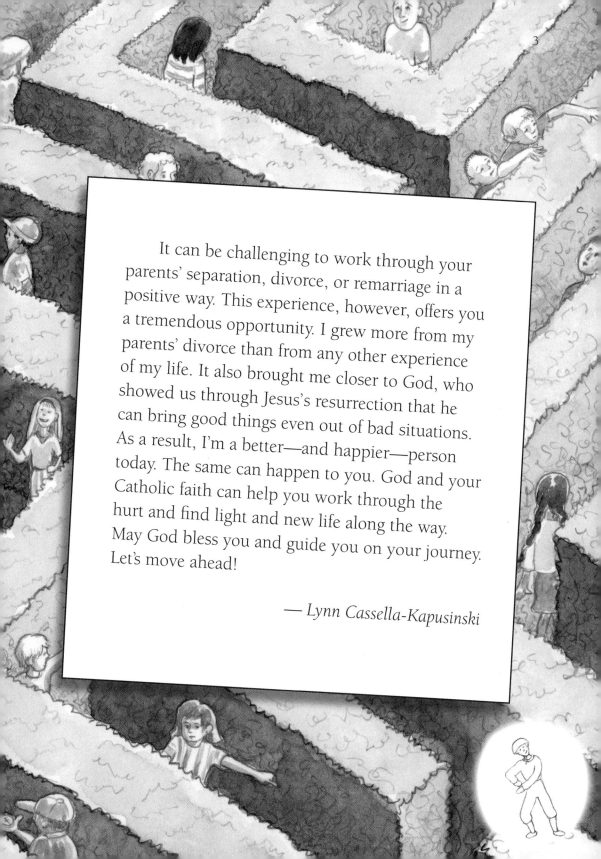

It can be challenging to work through your parents' separation, divorce, or remarriage in a positive way. This experience, however, offers you a tremendous opportunity. I grew more from my parents' divorce than from any other experience of my life. It also brought me closer to God, who showed us through Jesus's resurrection that he can bring good things even out of bad situations. As a result, I'm a better—and happier—person today. The same can happen to you. God and your Catholic faith can help you work through the hurt and find light and new life along the way. May God bless you and guide you on your journey. Let's move ahead!

— *Lynn Cassella-Kapusinski*

A Note to Parents
and Other Family Members

Dear Parents,

Thank you for your interest in using *When Parents Divorce or Separate* to help your child or children address the hurt and insecurity of separation, divorce, or remarriage. In working with parents over the years as a counselor; through my foundation, Faith Journeys; and from what my own parents have shared with me, I know that what you face is challenging, sometimes even overwhelming.

It can be difficult to acknowledge all that your child may be experiencing. Even in the best circumstances, this experience is one of grief and loss, but it doesn't have to remain only that. The good news is that the more a child is able to process this loss, the more good can come from it. That includes the possibility of your child's own happy marriage someday.

The key is to provide children with a safe space in which to work through their grief, and ample opportunity to do so. It is important that you respect your child's need for that space in order to heal. As difficult as it may be, please remember that this book belongs to your child. The decision to share what is inside also belongs to your child.

While the experience of separation or divorce can strain our faith, it is important to help children put it all together by drawing on their Catholic faith. That usually means answering their questions about Church teaching in the process. In this way, children can grow from their experience, not just in spite of it. The goal of this book is to help kids do precisely that.

When Parents Divorce or Separate assists kids in developing foundational skills such as effective communication, problem solving, anger management, and empathy. It also offers children a relevant faith perspective in service to the healing journey. As a result, your child will be better equipped not only to adjust to a family break-up or remarriage, but also to build their other relationships in a healthy and faith-filled way.

Whether your family's breakup is recent or years old, *When Parents Divorce or Separate* will assist your child in navigating what is often very tricky territory. Loss due to family breakup is often ambiguous, as divorce lacks the finality and closure that accompany other losses, most notably death. The fact that some things are lost and others stay the same can have the effect of freezing grief for the children in these circumstances.

Since children process and rework their losses at different levels as they mature, I recommend that you encourage them to work through this book on a regular basis. This approach provides the best opportunity to help kids keep from developing unhealthy coping skills and relationship patterns. It may also be helpful to return to this book whenever a related transition arises in your child's life. Moving, changes in custody arrangements, parental dating or remarriage, or the birth of a half-sibling often reopen old wounds.

The healing process for your child will probably take longer than you'd like. At the same time, you may find yourself replaying your own grief. In any case, it is important for you to give permission to your child to heal and grow at his or her own pace. That process may be longer—or shorter—than the path you take. It will necessarily be different.

Through it all, however, remember that the suffering of Jesus led to new life. So too can your child's pain, and your own, be transformed into something good and valuable. This is what our Catholic faith offers us: the grace to find meaning in suffering. Once we do, our pain can become growth; we can move past self-pity and recognize that—although things are really tough right now—we have the power and ability to make good choices. Realizing their hurts won't last forever, our children can accept help from others.

When children learn how to handle suffering with faith, a greatness is created inside them. It is my prayer that this book may be used as a healing instrument in your child's life. Always remember that "all things work together for good for those who love God, who are called according to his purpose" (Romans 8:28). May God bless you and your family!

— *Lynn Cassella-Kapusinski*

Please note that this book is not intended to replace the advice of psychologists or other healthcare professionals, but should be considered an additional resource. Questions and concerns about mental health should always be discussed with a healthcare provider.

Chapter One

Family

Do I Still Have One?
Will I Ever Have One Again?

Ethan wished he could crawl under a desk and hide. This was the worst assignment ever. Miss Jones, his social studies teacher, asked the class to create their own family crests. She told them to start by thinking of ideas and symbols that represented their family histories or lives. Before Miss Jones was finished giving the details, one of Ethan's classmates, Sam, had already drawn and colored his symbol. Miss Jones walked by Sam's desk and was so impressed that she asked him to show it to the class. He held up a red and blue yin-yang symbol from the South Korean flag. He said the symbol represented balance between opposites. Then he told the class that his family came to the United States when he was five years old and found many differences living here. Miss Jones said, "That's very interesting," and went on to observe that his symbol

6

could also mean balance or harmony. Natalie, another classmate, was so excited that she opened her backpack and took out pictures of her cousin's recent wedding in El Salvador. Miss Jones liked that idea too, and said it could represent joy.

But there was nothing about Ethan's family that he was happy about. Instead, he felt embarrassed and angry because his parents had separated a few months ago. Now, his mom was hardly ever home because she spent a lot more time at work. As a result, Ethan's aunt watched him and his younger brother on most days. Ethan saw his dad a whole lot less, too, just every other weekend from Saturday morning to Sunday afternoon.

The bell rang. Ethan's classmates quickly packed their things and lined up for lunch. Ethan shoved the assignment sheet into his backpack. *Another stupid assignment I probably just won't do,* he thought. He had been an okay student, but had lost interest in his schoolwork ever since his parents separated. He wished he could have a perfect family like the other kids. On some days, he even felt like he didn't have a family at all.

At dinner that night, after grace, Ethan's Aunt Dawn asked him about his homework. Ethan said he didn't have any but, after his aunt pressed him, Ethan told her about the assignment and why he couldn't do it.

His aunt put down her fork and said, "It can seem like you don't have a family anymore because of all the changes you've been through. But you're forgetting that the most important parts have stayed the same."

"Like what?" Ethan asked.

"Your love for one another," she told him. "Your parents are struggling a lot right now, but they still love you very much.

"A lot goes into making a family," she went on, "things like sharing, sacrificing, and helping with homework. It all boils down to love."

Ethan nodded. He had forgotten about his family's love for him. He didn't think much about his part in loving them, either.

"And there's your faith, too. God is still with all of you," his aunt said. "And the more you live in Christ and for Christ, the stronger your family will be."

Ethan realized his Aunt Dawn was right. "Thanks," he said, then got up from his chair and hugged her. He felt a lot better about his family now.

Your Family

Ethan felt embarrassed and angry about his family because of his parents' separation.

On some days, he even felt like he didn't have a family at all.

What are your thoughts or feelings about your family?

Write or draw a picture about them below.

my family

Facts About Families

1. There's no such thing as a perfect family.

   Like Ethan in the story, you may think others have a perfect family. But think about it: since no one is perfect, no family is perfect either. Instead, all families are imperfect because they're made up of imperfect people. We all have different personalities, as well as different strengths and weaknesses.

2. *All* families experience loss.

   Every family experiences loss at some point. For example, you may have a friend whose family member has died or is facing a serious illness. Or, you may know of someone whose parent has lost a job or left home to serve in the military. Families can face losses that are the result of natural disasters or having to move far away, too. All of these situations challenge us to accept and adjust to a loss. Your parents' separation, divorce, or remarriage means adjusting to a loss, too.

3. A separation or divorce affects all family members, but in different ways.

   While you might feel sad or mad, your brother or sister may feel frightened, your grandparents may feel disappointed, and your parents may

feel lonely. All these feelings are normal. Because every one of us is unique, we should expect that our family members might experience their losses in different ways.

Similarities and Differences

Ethan's aunt pointed out that some things change and some things stay the same when parents separate or divorce.

On the diagram below, note the similarities and differences for your family.

If you need help, see Ethan's diagram below.

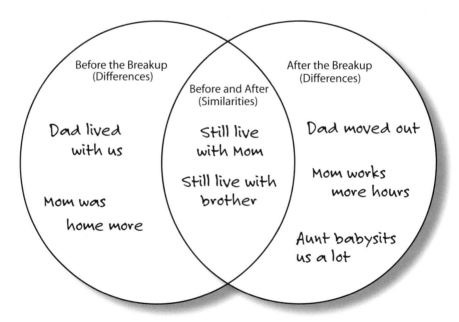

Before the Breakup
(Differences)

Before and After
(Similarities)

After the Breakup
(Differences)

Dad lived
with us

Still live
with Mom

Dad moved out

Still live with
brother

Mom works
more hours

Mom was
home more

Aunt babysits
us a lot

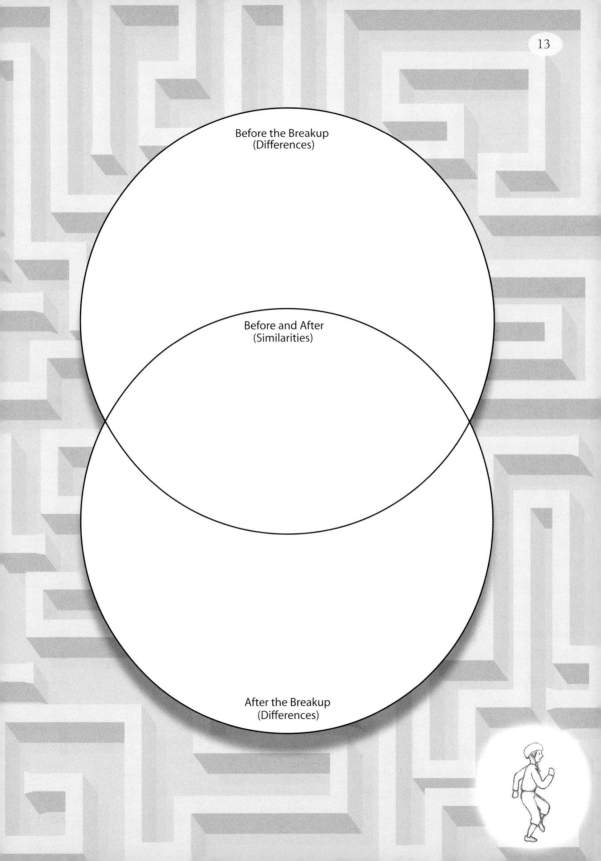

Before the Breakup
(Differences)

Before and After
(Similarities)

After the Breakup
(Differences)

Difficult Changes ▸▸▸▸▸▸▸▸▸▸▸▸

Look back at the changes you just noted in activity 2.

Which changes are hardest for you to accept?

Write about or draw a picture of one of those changes below.

4 Your Family's Love for You

Ethan's aunt emphasized one thing that stays the same after separation or divorce: a family's love for one another.

In what ways does your family show love to you? Check off the ways (below) that apply to you.

▼ ▼ ▼ ▼ ▼ ▼ ▼ ▼ ▼ ▼ ▼ ▼ ▼

_____ Helping me with homework

_____ Sharing their things (e.g., games, clothes, art supplies, etc.)

_____ Taking care of me when I'm sick

_____ Giving me a hug or kiss

_____ Sharing in my interests and hobbies

_____ Accepting my differences

_____ Listening when I'm talking

_____ Helping me with problems

_____ Providing for me financially

_____ Letting me have a say in family decisions

_____ Encouraging me

_____ Other. Please explain.

_____

Things to Remember

The Fourth Commandment

In the Fourth Commandment, God tells us to "Honor your father and your mother, so that your days may be long in the land which the LORD your God is giving you" (Exodus 20:12; Deuteronomy 5:16). This commandment also includes our relationships with other family members and relatives. Therefore, we are commanded to love our brothers and sisters, help them, treat them with respect, and accept their faults. We may find it easier to accept someone else's faults when we are able to admit that we have faults of our own.

It can be difficult to honor your parents if you are angry at them, or if they have hurt or disappointed you. Sometimes, parents act terribly, and that makes it hard to honor them too. Honoring does not mean that you need to ignore your feelings. Nor does it mean you have to excuse your parents' behavior. Instead, honoring means treating your parents with consideration and trying to forgive them.

The Fourth Commandment also tells us to obey other authorities, such as teachers, older people, and the Church.

A Domestic Church

The family is so important that it's called to be a domestic church or a church in the home. This is because most kids first learn about prayer and God's love from their family. By showing love to your family and practicing Christian virtues (holy habits such as patience, kindness, and charity), you help to build a small church in your home.

Your family may have been damaged by separation or divorce, but it is still a family. There is no hurt that is too big for God to heal.

You are always part of God's family.

As a Christian, you also belong to God's family. This happened at your Baptism when you became a member of the Church, the body of Christ. The Church is the community of people who are baptized followers of Jesus Christ. As a result of your Baptism, you are united with all Christians through the workings of the Holy Spirit, and you have millions of brothers and sisters in Christ!

Loving Your Family

Ethan seemed to forget about his part in loving his family members.

How could you do a better job of loving your family members?

Write your answer below.

(Examples: showing more respect to my parents and/or siblings, doing extra chores, looking after a younger sibling, apologizing when I'm wrong, understanding another's point of view, telling family members I love them, and so on.)

_____

_____

_____

_____

_____

_____

_____

_____

_____

_____

Living in and for Christ

Ethan's aunt pointed out that God was still with him and his family too.

Below are ways to remember God at home.
Check off all the things you will try.

_____ Pray with my family at meals

_____ Say the Rosary together

_____ Make a shrine to Jesus or the Blessed Mother in my home or yard

_____ Celebrate the date of my Baptism with my godparents

_____ Place statues or pictures of Jesus or the Blessed Mother in my bedroom or living room

_____ Read the Bible together

_____ Attend Mass together

_____ Place a holy water font by our front door

_____ Celebrate the feast day of the saint I was named after

_____ Read about the saints and holy days noted on a calendar and discuss them

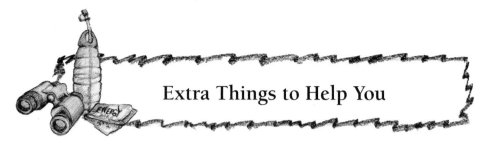

Extra Things to Help You

🐦 Look back at the section "Facts About Families." Choose one and write about how it applies to your family, or draw a picture that shows how it applies.

🐌 Set aside a day (or part of a day) to do something someone in your family wants to do. For example, maybe your dad or sister enjoys watching a certain sports team on TV. Or, perhaps your mom or brother enjoys planting flowers. Join your family member in this activity, even if it's not what you like to do. You'll notice your relationship to that person grow closer as a result.

🐟 Surprise your parent or sibling with a special note. It can be a thank-you note, one that says "I love you," or a note to let them know you're thinking of them during a stressful time. Put the note where your family member will be sure to see it (for example, in a backpack, briefcase, or purse). They'll likely appreciate your thoughtfulness.

🐜 In addition to showing extra consideration toward a family member, consider doing something to help someone in your community. For example, you could participate in a food and/or clothing drive at your school or church, volunteer at a soup kitchen, or do some other community service project. When we help those less fortunate, it can remind us of the blessings we have (such as our own families).

 Ask your mom or dad if you can have a family meeting at least once a month in each home. This can be a special time set aside with either your mom or dad to discuss matters that affect you and your siblings. After the meeting, your parents can then discuss any important concerns or decisions that have to be finalized. A family meeting can include assigning chores, deciding how the holidays will be spent, or more serious matters like how to handle an illness of a relative or a change in family finances. The meeting can be used to share positives too, such as what's going well in your family. Family meetings can do a lot to strengthen your family.

PRAYER

Lord, I'm struggling. My family has changed in ways I'm finding hard to accept. Give me your peace, and the grace to understand that no one's family is perfect. Help me recognize that everyone has limitations. Show me, and all my family members, how to adjust to what has happened. Teach me how to love the members of my family more, and to be more grateful for the ways they show their love for me. You have the power to bring good from every situation. Help me to grow from this experience. Amen.

Take Aways

Write down two or three things in this chapter that you'd like to remember or think will help you the most.

1. _____

2. _____

3. _____

Chapter Two

Crummy Feelings

What Do You Do with Them?

When Hailey's stepdad moved out and she learned her mom was getting a second divorce, Hailey had many different feelings. At first, she felt relieved because she wouldn't hear them fight so much. Soon after, though, her mind filled with questions about the changes this divorce would bring. *How often will I see my stepdad? Can I still go to the same school? What am I going to tell my friends? Will they still be my friends?* Hailey felt embarrassed and worried. Then she felt mad, especially at her mom and at God. One divorce was bad enough. She shouldn't have to go through it a second time. Hailey really liked her stepdad a lot too. He had been like a real father to her, and now he was leaving. *None of this is fair,* she thought.

Hailey didn't like what she was feeling. She tried to ignore them, but the feelings grew. She got so mad

that she slammed her bedroom door and began to cry. Later, she refused to leave her room and eat dinner.

That evening, Hailey heard a knock on her door. "Hailey," her mom called. "I'd like to talk with you."

Hailey slowly opened the door, then sat down on her bed. She hugged her legs tight in front of her. Her face felt very hot.

Hailey's mom closed the door. "You look really mad," she said.

"I am mad," Hailey said, "and confused." Then Hailey asked the questions she had about the divorce, and her mom answered them. Hailey's mom also explained that changes like divorce bring losses that can make someone feel many different feelings. She called these feelings grief, and said they go up and down like waves in the ocean. She also said it was important to get grief out in a safe way. Otherwise, it could come out in ways that could be hurtful to herself or others.

Hailey and her mom discussed good ways to express grief feelings. Since Hailey enjoyed drawing, she decided to draw whenever she got upset about the divorce. She figured it would help to keep talking with her mom too.

Hailey started to feel better. She still didn't like the divorce and still had questions for God. However, it helped a lot to know that there was something she could do with her crummy feelings.

 **1 Your Feelings**

Hailey had many different feelings about her mom's second divorce.

Some of those feelings conflicted with her other feelings.

This happened when she felt relieved, then worried.

What feelings do you have about your parents' separation or divorce?

Describe or draw a picture that explains how you feel, such as:

sad

lonely

glad

mad

scared

worried

Or, explain two conflicting feelings that you have.

_____

_____

_____

_____

_____

Sorting It Out

Feelings are a natural and important part of who we are. As you probably already experienced, though, feelings can become overwhelming when parents separate, divorce, or remarry. Perhaps this has caused you to shut down and not express feelings as a result. If you've done that, it may cause you more harm than good. Why? Because your emotions—feelings like anger and sadness—can become like a quiet volcano that later erupts, hurting others as well as yourself.

The sooner you express and sort through your feelings, the better. It's also important to learn about feelings and do your best to label them correctly.

Remember to take a break from this work, too. Continue to do things you enjoy, like spending time with your friends or playing sports. Even when you are grieving, it's still okay to have fun!

Sad or Lonely

It's natural to feel sad or lonely when parents separate or divorce because many losses result from the breakup. It takes courage to accept and face these losses, but the more you work at doing so, the better you will feel in the long run. Sometimes, facing losses also means feeling so sad or lonely that you cry. You might be tempted to think that crying is just for babies, or that holding back your tears shows that you are strong. But that isn't true. Allowing yourself to cry is not only okay; it's one of the best things you can do to help yourself heal. Usually, your sad or lonely feelings will lessen with time if you find a healthy way to get them out. However, for a really big loss, there may always be a little bit of sadness left.

Mad

Like Hailey in the story, you may feel angry because you feel the divorce isn't fair. It may seem even more unfair when you see your friends whose parents aren't divorced because those friends may get to do more with their parents than you do. It is true that separation and divorce are unfair, especially for kids. They can make growing up more difficult. You may have good reason to be mad, but that doesn't mean anyone intended to hurt you. It is important that you don't take the anger you feel out on other people, or on yourself.

Feeling angry can be a sign that there is something else going on inside us. Often underneath a lot of anger is hurt. We often try to push away hurt feelings and feel mad instead. That's because being angry can make us feel stronger, more in control, or grown up. It's okay to feel mad, but try to dig a little deeper to unearth those hurt feelings. Discovering what hurts underneath can do a lot to help you heal.

Jealous

In addition to feeling jealous of your friends whose parents are still married, you may also feel jealous of your mom's or dad's attention, especially if either of your parents starts to date.

Remembering a few things can help. First, no family is perfect, not even families with two happily married parents. So, while it may seem like your friends have it better than you, you may enjoy some benefit with your family that your friends do not. The more you are able to work through the crummy feelings that come with your parents' divorce, the more good you will be able to take from that not-so-good situation.

Second, the way we see or feel about something isn't always the way it really is. While it may seem like you're getting less of your parent's love if your mom or dad starts dating, that's not necessarily true. In fact, the reverse might happen. The love your

parent has for you is a special kind of love, different from any other. That love won't become less, even if your parent's love for someone else grows.

You might still feel jealous, though, if your mom or dad really is spending more time with a new dating partner than with you. If that's what's happening, speak up and find a way to tell your parent how you feel and what you want. For example, "I know your girlfriend is important to you, Dad, but I feel like you're forgetting me. Could you and I do things by ourselves sometimes, like go to a movie or out to lunch? It would help me feel a lot better." That kind of honesty and respect is what builds family relationships.

Guilty

Adults cause separation and divorce, not kids. Still, many kids feel guilty when their parents separate or divorce. Why? Because when we blame ourselves, it can give us a false sense of control over bad things that happen. If you feel guilty, remember that there's nothing you said or did that caused the breakup. There's also nothing you can say or do that can make your parents get back together. Separation and divorce are and always will be an adult problem.

Even if you've heard your parents mention you in an argument, remember that their breakup is not your fault. Instead, your parents may argue because they cannot work together about matters that involve you. Things such as discipline or how money is spent are challenges for every family.

Scared or Worried

There are lots of reasons why your parents' separation or divorce might make you feel scared or worried. One may be because you can't be with one (or both) of your parents as much. When that happens, it can feel like you're losing one or even both of your parents. That really isn't true. Time or distance apart doesn't mean that your parents love you less than they did before. Remember, your parents are divorcing each other; they're not divorcing you!

Sometimes, kids feel scared or worried because they fear one or both of their parents won't be strong enough to get through the divorce. Maybe you've noticed changes in a parent's behavior that upset you. Perhaps your parent is sleeping more than usual, or looks sad or stressed a lot of the time. Maybe your house isn't as clean as usual, or meals aren't as good as they used to be. If so, share your feelings and concerns with your parent. For example, you could say something like, "I'm scared because you seem sad a lot. Are you okay?" You could also write your parent a note about your concerns, if that would be easier.

It can be scary and worrisome when you're not sure what other changes the divorce will bring to

your life. If this is how you feel, ask your mom and dad any questions you have. Be sure to tell them what you want too. You may not always get it, but your parents will at least be more aware of how you see things. And if there's something you need to work on, like an unrealistic expectation, this kind of honest and open communication can help you in other ways as well.

"I Thought I Was Over This."

At times you may be surprised by how you feel. Even when you think you're past most of your crummy feelings, holidays, birthdays, and other special occasions can trigger your grief all over again. This is normal, especially if one of your parents can't be there to celebrate with you. If this happens, don't be hard on yourself! Recognize that this is just another step in the healing process, and sort out your feel-ings again.

Feelings and Your Body

Feelings affect the body. In the story, Hailey got so mad that her face felt hot. When you're angry, you may feel your heart beat faster. When you're nervous, your mouth might get dry.

On the drawing below, color where you feel your feelings.

Use these colors:

Guilty = Purple

Happy = Yellow

Jealous = Green

Lonely = Brown

Mad = Red

Relieved = Tan/Gold

Sad = Blue

Scared = Black

Worried = Orange

Other feeling = You choose the color.

Your Body's "Alarm"

Feelings can affect the body in more serious ways too, especially if you don't express them and keep them locked inside instead. If you do this, your body may react by sounding its "alarm." You may get a headache or stomachache. Or you may over-eat or sleep more than usual. The reverse can happen too. Some people don't feel like eating or have trouble sleeping. All of these responses are signals that your feelings need more attention than you're giving them.

If your parents separated recently, these physical reactions are more common. However, if it's been a few months or longer, and your body is still sounding its alarm, tell your parents or a trusted adult right away so you can get the extra help you may need.

The Waves of Grief

In the story, Hailey's mom said that grief feelings go up and down like waves in the ocean.

Draw your "grief waves" below. Describe what happens when your grief goes up and down.

Here's an example:

Hear kids at school talk about something fun they did with their dad; I start missing Dad.

Go to baseball practice and Dad isn't there.

Saying prayers, mad at God for letting divorce happen.

wake up   busy at school   doing homework   sleeping

Here is a picture of my grief waves.

4 Helping Yourself

In the story, Hailey thought of a plan for getting her feelings out in a healthy way.
Her plan included drawing and talking with her mom.

Check off all the ways you will try to get your feelings out.

_____ Draw

_____ Write in a journal

_____ Write a note to God

_____ Pray and/or talk to God

_____ Talk with another child who has separated or divorced parents

_____ Talk to one or both of your parents

_____ Talk with a counselor

_____ Talk with good friends.
Write their names here.

_____

_____

_____

_____ Play a sport

_____ Do another physical activity (for example,
ride my bike, run with my dog, dance)

_____ Clean, organize, or fix something

_____ Play a musical instrument

_____ Sing

_____ Cry

_____ Punch or yell into a pillow or ball

_____ Do you have other ways to get feelings out?
Draw or write them on this page.

Facts About Feelings

1. A healthy way to respond to feelings is to identify what they are, admit that you have them, and try to work through them. This is called grieving. An unhealthy way to respond is to pretend you don't have feelings, or to take them out on someone else.

2. The more you accept your feelings—and face them—the more you will heal.

3. Talking with someone about your feelings does not make them disappear. It can, however, help you feel better.

4. Bottling up your feelings hardly ever makes them get better. More often, it can make you feel worse.

5. Like Hailey in the story, you may have mixed or conflicting feelings about your parents' separation or divorce. For example, maybe one day you feel relieved, then the next day you feel sad, and the third day you feel like you don't care. Is that okay? Definitely. There is no right way to feel when parents separate or divorce.

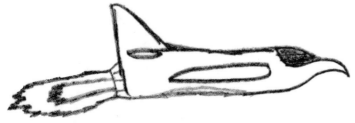

What Our Church Teaches

Our faith tells us that it is important to take care of our feelings. Why? Because that's how to prevent them from getting the best of us. When we learn how to deal with crummy feelings in positive ways, we will be free to accomplish all we are capable of and build positive and healthy relationships with others. By becoming what God made us to be, we bring honor and glory to him. This is the most important thing we can do because it is the reason God created each one of us.

Here's more of what our Church has to say about feelings:

1. Passions, or strong feelings, are good when they help us do something good, but evil when they encourage us to do something wrong (*Catechism of the Catholic Church*, 1768). Are your feelings encouraging you to do good or to sin by turning away from God and the law he has given us?

2. There is another important reason to make sure our feelings are influencing us to do good: The more we do what is good, the more free we become.

3. Feelings themselves are neither moral nor immoral —that is, they are not right or wrong. Therefore, it is incorrect to believe that anger, sadness, and

other "negative" feelings are "bad" or immoral feelings. Instead, *how we act* when we are angry, sad, jealous, and the like can be right or wrong. Actions, not feelings, can be sinful.

Extra Things to Help You

1. Empathy builder: Understanding your own feelings better will help you understand the feelings of others. This is called *empathy* (EM-path-ee). When you can set your own feelings aside for a bit and are ready to practice empathy, try answering these questions:

a) How do you think each of your family members feels about the separation or divorce? Write down their names (below) and the feelings beside it. If you're not sure, write "not sure" beside their names.

_____

_____

_____

_____

_____

b) Does anyone in your family have feelings that seem similar to yours? If so, explain how the feelings are similar. (For example, I feel sad. My sister seems sad too because she doesn't spend as much time with her friends as she used to. She stays in her room a lot more now.)

_____

_____

_____

c) Does anyone in your family have feelings that are different from yours? If so, explain how the feelings are different. (For example, I am still very angry at my dad and don't want to talk with him. My brother, though, has forgiven him and gets along well with him.)

_____

_____

_____

 2. Look over the "Facts About Feelings" section on page 38 and choose one of them. Explain or draw a picture (below) that shows what you think or how you feel about the fact you chose.

3. Feelings circles: What feelings did you have during the past week about your parents' separation, divorce, or remarriage?

a) Draw one circle below for each feeling.

b) Write the name of the feeling inside the circle.

c) Color the circle to show how much time you had that feeling (you can use the colors from activity 2 on page 33). How can you work through those feelings?

PRAYER

Lord, I know that you are with me when I'm feeling
good. Show me that you are also with me when I feel

_____, _____, _____.

(List your crummy feelings here.)

Your Son Jesus accepted his cross. Help me to accept the way
I feel. Give me the grace of self-control, and teach me how
to express my emotions in healthy ways. Guide me when I
make choices. Strengthen me with the courage I need to work
through my feelings. Lead me to healing and peace, Lord, and
help me to grow from this experience. For you have the power
to bring good from every situation. Amen.

Take Aways

Write down two or three things in this chapter that you'd
like to remember or think will help you the most.

1.

2.

3.

Separation and Divorce

Why Does It Happen?

Seth hit the soccer ball with his hand and scored a goal. His teammates raised their arms and cheered.

"No way!" Ryan shouted. He ran over to the ball, picked it up, and held it tight with both arms.

"It counts!" Seth exclaimed. He walked closer to Ryan. "The score is now two to one," he added.

"You're not the goalie," Ryan said. "You can't hit the ball with your hands. That's against the rules." He moved the ball to his side, away from Seth.

"Put the ball down," Seth demanded. "We have to kick off from the center."

"No," Ryan said. "It's our ball now. We kick off from the goal box," he added. He turned and pointed to it.

Just then, Seth punched the ball out of Ryan's arm, then kicked the ball away from Ryan. He and his team ran after it.

"Hey," Ryan shouted, "that's not fair."

The boys on Seth's team started laughing.

Ryan called out to the aftercare teacher, "Mrs. Bergman, they're cheating!"

"Work it out among yourselves," she said.

"I tried, but it didn't work," Ryan told her.

Mrs. Bergman shook her head and looked away.

It's probably not going to work out for my parents either, Ryan thought. He remembered the last time he heard them talking. They were discussing their final divorce hearing. Even though he knew about that and it had been almost two years since the separation, Ryan still didn't want to believe a divorce could really happen.

Mrs. Bergman got up and blew her whistle. "Line up, everyone!" she shouted. "It's time for snack."

Ryan walked slowly to the line. He didn't feel like eating. His stomach felt like one big ball of fear. Question after question kept pounding in his head. *What really made Dad file for the divorce anyway? Did he even try to work things out with Mom?* Then Ryan wondered, *maybe if I do more chores Mom and Dad won't be so stressed, and they'll get along better. I could try harder to get better grades in school too. That might make them happier.*

Later that night, just before he went to sleep, Ryan talked with his dad. "I have a suggestion," he said.

"Okay," his dad said. "Let's hear it."

Ryan sat up on his bed and said, "I think it'd be good for me to do more chores, both here and at Mom's house."

His dad raised his eyebrows. "Great idea, but that would mean you'd have to finish the chores you already have first, and we both know how often that happens. Time to get to sleep now," his dad said and turned off the light.

"No, wait!" Ryan blurted out.

His dad turned the light back on.

"I-I think it would help," Ryan forced out, "you know, with the stress."

"Yes, it probably would," his dad answered. "Your mother and I both work long hours."

"I mean, with the divorce," Ryan added. "Maybe, if you were less stressed out you'd get along better," Ryan blurted out. "And maybe you could call off the divorce and —"

His dad took a deep breath.

"Why does the divorce have to happen?" Ryan asked. He felt his eyes well up with tears.

"This is really between your mother and me," his dad said.

"But it affects me!" Ryan shouted.

"Someday, when you're older," his dad said, "I'll explain everything to you."

Ryan thrust himself down on the bed and turned away from his dad. Ryan felt so mad he wanted to scream. *Dad caused this whole mess*, Ryan thought. *And now he's hurting me more by keeping secrets.*

"Let's get to sleep now," his dad said. "We have to get up early tomorrow to go to Grandma and Grandpa's house."

His dad turned out the lights. "Good night," he said, then closed the door.

Getting Parents Back Together

Ryan wanted to get his parents back together!
He thought he could bring this about by doing
more chores and getting better grades.
Do you ever feel like this?

Write or draw a picture about your answer below.

What Caused the Separation or Divorce?

Ryan didn't understand the reasons why his parents were getting divorced.

Do you have any questions about what caused your parents' separation or divorce?

If so, write or draw a picture about them below.

Sorting It Out

Ryan felt more angry and embarrassed at the end of the story because his questions about why his parents were divorcing were not answered.

Couples separate and divorce for many reasons.

Some of those reasons are explained below.

Put a star beside any reason that describes your parents' situation.

If you're not sure, put a question mark beside the reason.

• • • • • • Reasons Why Parents May • • • • • • • • • • Separate or Divorce

_____Poor Communication

If you play a team sport, you know how important it is to communicate with your teammates so that the players work together and do their very best. Communication is an essential part of all other relationships too–

especially marriage. Sometimes, though, couples find it difficult to talk about and work through their disagreements in a healthy way. Or, they may get so busy with other priorities that they don't set aside time to talk and share with one another as much as they need to. In either situation, a husband and wife can grow distant from each other, and hurt feelings can build up over time.

_____Financial Problems

Money is a common cause of stress in a marriage. A couple might argue about how their money should be spent, or have very different spending or saving habits. Sometimes, one spouse may spend money without telling the other. Or it may become harder to pay bills if one spouse loses a job. That can put a lot of strain on a marriage too. If a couple cannot discuss and resolve their financial problems, they may decide to divorce.

_____Differences in Values

The importance we place on different things reflects our **values**. Values play a major role in how we live our lives, and in how we share our lives with others. A conflict of values or priorities can cause serious problems in a marriage. For example, one spouse may place a lot of importance on social status and want to spend money on lavish vacations, an expensive home, and going out often. The other spouse may value a simpler lifestyle, preferring to stay at home most of the time and save as much money as possible. A couple might divorce if they cannot find a way to resolve these differences.

_____Infidelity or Unfaithfulness

No one can take the place of a husband or wife. **Infidelity**, sometimes called "cheating," occurs when one spouse seeks inappropriate companionship outside the marriage. While it is good for husbands and wives to have other friends, they should not let another person become more important to them than their spouse is. If this happens, the other relationship causes a lot of hurt and harms the unity between husband and wife.

_____Immaturity

When people aren't grown up enough to make a very important decision like marriage, they might not be able to know themselves or each other well enough yet to decide if they are a good fit for each other. When immature couples marry, they may also not be fully aware of the responsibilities marriage involves.

_____Addictions or Substance Abuse

An **addiction** is a strong desire or craving for something that is hard for a person to control or stop. You may know about drug addiction or alcohol abuse. But people can also become addicted to other things like food, or behaviors such as gambling. When a person has an addiction, physical health and the health of his or her family relationships are at risk. If addiction or substance abuse is part of a married person's life, the marriage suffers and may end in divorce. In all these situations, both the person with the addiction and his or her family need professional help to recover.

_____Physical, Verbal, or Emotional Abuse

You probably know that bullying is wrong. People who tease, hurt, or threaten others often do so in order to gain power over them. Sometimes, however, husbands and wives may bully or abuse each other, or their children. **Abuse** can be physical, such as hitting; verbal, such as shouting or insulting; or emotional, such as intimidating or ignoring someone. When this abuse is serious or happens often, it can lead to divorce.

_____Mental Illness

A mental illness is a disease of the mind. It affects a person's thinking, feelings, and/or behavior and can make handling everyday situations difficult. As a result, a mental illness can cause a lot of stress in a marriage. Usually, a person with a mental illness needs to see a psychologist or psychiatrist routinely, and may take medication in order to live a healthier and more stable life. If people with mental illness don't take care of themselves and get the help they need, though, it can lead to addiction, abuse, financial difficulties, or other problems.

Taking Sides

Ryan blamed his dad for causing the divorce. Are you blaming one of your parents and taking your other parent's side?

If yes, read fact 1 on the next page, then write or draw your response to it below.

If no, choose another fact and write or draw your response to it.

My response to "Facts About Separation and Divorce"

Facts About Separation and Divorce

1. Divorce is rarely caused by just one spouse's mistakes.

Even if the divorce seems to be the fault of only one of your parents, that is rarely the case. Usually, both spouses made mistakes along the way, or perhaps they were not fully prepared when making the decision to marry in the first place.

2. Blame doesn't help.

Lots of situations can make us angry when parents separate or divorce. At times, those things can even tempt us to blame one parent for everything that has gone wrong.

Maybe one of your parents isn't spending as much time with you as before because he or she moved away, is working longer hours, began dating, or is feeling really sad. Or maybe your family can't go on vacation, or you can't buy as many things as you used to because there's less money. If one of your parents is very upset with the other, or if you feel closer to one of your parents than you do to the other, these things can influence you to take sides.

With all these situations, it can be easy to take one parent's side and blame the other who seems to be causing all the trouble. That's often unfair, though, and rarely the whole truth. Both your parents made the decision to marry. Usually, both also have some part in the decision to separate or divorce.

If you're blaming one of your parents, try to find out more about what caused the separation or divorce. It may help you treat the parent you're blaming more fairly. Remember, the goal is to love both your parents, and to be able to forgive them, too.

3. Divorce is never a kid's fault.

Are you blaming yourself for your parents' separation or divorce? If so, it may be because it helps you feel more in control, perhaps in control enough for you to believe that you can "fix" things. But the truth is that separation and divorce result from grown-up matters such as communication problems, differences in values, substance abuse, and other issues. Even if your parents argue about something that involves you (like how to pay for your education or how you should be disciplined), you are never the cause of their problems.

4. Kids can't make parents get back together.

You may make the mistake of thinking that there is something you can do to make your parents get back together. It's true that doing what your parents ask of you, like homework and chores, contributes to a happier and more peaceful home. Still, your parents' separation or divorce was caused by grown-up problems. It's hard to accept, but there really is nothing you can say or do to bring them back together.

5. It is irresponsible to use the divorce as an excuse.

When something else in your life doesn't go well, such as getting a bad grade or getting into trouble, it can be easy to blame your parents' separation or divorce. To be fair, your parents' breakup *can* make it more difficult to concentrate or handle upset feelings in a positive way. But while no one expects you to handle the divorce perfectly, you do need to try your best. Not trying means using the divorce as an excuse to avoid taking responsibility for your actions. You'll find that won't help you feel better.

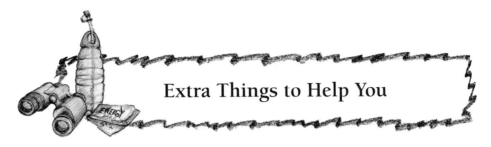

Extra Things to Help You

Look back at any question marks you noted in activity 3. Then, ask one or both of your parents if the reason applies to their situation. If they won't discuss this with you, try asking an older family member.

Interview a married couple that seem happily married. Ask them what makes their marriage work.

PRAYER

Lord, sometimes I just wish that I could fix everything, even things that aren't mine to fix. Keep me from feeling responsible for my parents' separation or divorce. Forgive me for the times I've taken sides, or did something to hurt my mom or dad because I was angry or wanted to be in control. Teach me how to learn from my parents' mistakes, and give me the grace to avoid making the same mistakes in my life. You have the power to bring good from every situation. Help me to grow from this experience.

Amen.

Take Aways

Write down two or three things in this chapter that you'd like to remember or think will help you the most.

1.

2.

3.

Chapter Four

Divorce Problems

What Can I Do to Help Solve Them?

Mr. Davolio, one of the lunchroom teachers, walked to the front of the cafeteria and blew his whistle. Once everyone quieted down, he made an announcement. "Anyone interested in trying out for the talent show must go to the music room now."

A bunch of kids shot up from their seats. Some rushed to return their lunch trays, while others threw out their trash.

Nicole continued eating her sandwich. She stared down at the lunch table. She was disappointed and angry. She really wanted to perform in the talent show, but after her parents' big argument on the phone last night, she had decided not to. Ever since her parents divorced, all they seemed to do was fight. The last thing she wanted was for them to fight at her school.

Nicole shoved her half-eaten sandwich into her lunch bag. *My parents should have waited until the end of the school year to get divorced,* she thought. *They know how important it is to me to perform at the talent show.*

Nicole's best friend, Monica, tapped Nicole on the shoulder. "Hurry up," Monica said, "you need to go to the music room."

"I'm not trying out," Nicole said.

"What do you mean?" Monica said. "You've been practicing for months."

"I changed my mind," Nicole said. She got up and threw the rest of her lunch into the garbage can.

Monica hurried after her. "I thought you were all excited about playing that song on the piano."

"I was," Nicole said, "but not anymore. Not with both my parents there."

"What's wrong with that?" Monica asked.

"Monica, you don't understand. They fight *all* the time," Nicole said. "I don't want them fighting here too." She stormed away and slumped herself back down at the lunch table.

Monica sat down next to her. "You can't just drop out of the talent show."

Nicole rolled her eyes at Monica. "It's no big deal."

"Yes it is," Monica said. "You should tell your parents how you feel. If they knew you were going to drop out, maybe they would promise not to fight."

"No, they'll never change," Nicole said. *No matter what I do, it won't change anything,* she thought. *Besides, I don't want to deal with this. And I shouldn't have to. They're supposed to be the adults.*

Common Reactions

How do you react when faced with a problem related to your parents' separation or divorce? If you're like Nicole, you might ignore the problem, try not to think about it, or tell yourself "it's no big deal." You might even try to distract yourself by being helpful to others instead. Or, maybe you get so angry about the problem that it causes you to take out your feelings on a sibling, teacher, classmate, or the parent you're living with. While these reactions look very different from one another, they all show a resistance to solving problems. It's not unusual to struggle in this way when faced with problems related to your parents' separation or divorce.

I Don't Want to Deal with This!

Nicole didn't want to deal with the problems resulting from her parents' divorce.

She also felt she shouldn't have to because her parents were the adults and should have known better.

How do you feel about solving problems related to your parents' separation or divorce?

Write or draw a picture about this below.

Ignoring problems or resisting having to deal with them may seem to help in the short run, but it's not an effective way to solve problems or improve things in the long run. In fact, problems that aren't addressed when they come up can become even worse problems down the road.

So even though you're not responsible for your parents' separation or divorce, you are responsible for helping yourself through it. That includes trying to do something positive about whatever problems you may be having as a result.

There are a few important points to remember:

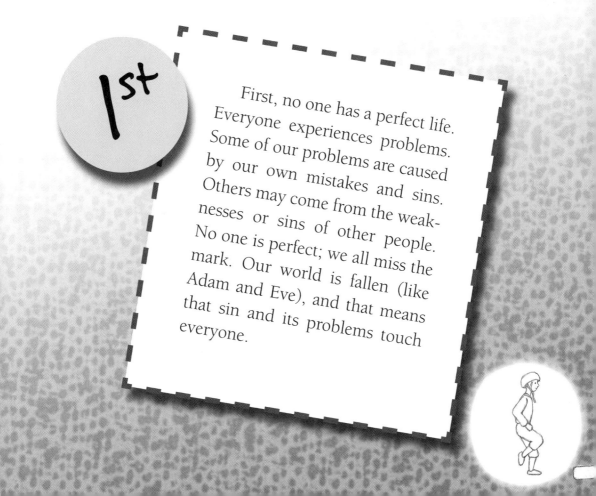

1st

First, no one has a perfect life. Everyone experiences problems. Some of our problems are caused by our own mistakes and sins. Others may come from the weaknesses or sins of other people. No one is perfect; we all miss the mark. Our world is fallen (like Adam and Eve), and that means that sin and its problems touch everyone.

2ⁿᵈ

Second, although you may wish you didn't have to face the problems you have, they do provide you with something good: an opportunity to grow as a person. It's like getting an extra-credit homework assignment. You don't have to do it. But if you choose to do the extra work you'll get extra credit and be better prepared for the next test. As you work through your parents' separation or divorce, you will become more ready to solve other problems that come your way in the future.

3ʳᵈ

Finally, remember that solving problems is rarely easy. It often requires hard work. The good news, though, is that most problems can be solved, solving them can make your life a whole lot better, and you don't have to solve them alone. Here are some exercises to help you get there.

Identifying the Problem

Nicole's parents were fighting a lot. As a result, she didn't want them to attend her school events together.

What problems are your parents' separation or divorce causing you?

List them below and try to be as specific as possible.

Then, draw a star next to your biggest problem.

_____

_____

_____

_____

_____

_____

What Is Your Goal?

Nicole had a goal: She wanted to perform in the talent show without worrying that her parents might start fighting.

Consider the biggest problem you identified in activity 2.

What improvement or change would you like to see?

Write it down below. Be as specific as possible.

to the moon and back!

Divorce Solutions

Nicole handled her problem by dropping out of the talent show.

However, this solution did not help her achieve her goal.

Monica suggested another solution: that Nicole talk with her parents about how she felt, and what she wanted.

How could you achieve your goal?

(It can help to think of successful ways you have solved other problems in the past.)

List as many solutions as you can think of below.

_____

_____

_____

_____

_____

_____

Solution Outcomes

Nicole's solution had positive and negative consequences, or outcomes.

However, the negative outcomes outweighed the positive ones.

Here's one way to tell the difference. A positive outcome leaves you feeling more at peace with yourself and others. A negative one will make you feel the opposite.

What could be the possible outcomes of your solutions (noted in activity 4)?

Are they positive or negative?

Complete the chart on the next page for each solution.

Example

Divorce Solution	Possible Positive Outcome	Possible Negative Outcome
Drop out of talent show	Parents can't fight that way	I can't perform, and I want to
Talk to parents about my problem	They may realize how I feel and may try harder not to fight. Then, I could perform in the talent show and not be embarrassed.	They could get upset with me
Ask only one parent to attend the talent show	Parents can't fight that way	I might hurt the feelings of the parent whom I don't invite

Outcomes of My Solution(s)

Divorce Solution	Possible Positive Outcome	Possible Negative Outcome

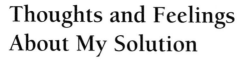

Thoughts and Feelings About My Solution

Nicole didn't want to try another solution because she thought her parents would never change.

Based on what you discovered in activity 5, what do you think is your best solution?

What do you think and how do you feel about trying it?

My best solution is:

_____

_____

_____

_____

My thoughts and feelings about trying it are:

_____

_____

_____

_____

_____

Sometimes, when we're trying to solve problems, the way we think about them can get in the way. Our thoughts can become an even bigger difficulty than the divorce problem we're trying so hard to solve!

For example, Nicole thought her problem couldn't be solved because she assumed her parents couldn't change and stop fighting. Those thoughts prevented her from even trying to solve her problem.

When we are experiencing negative things in our lives, it can be hard to think about them in a positive way. Instead, we can end up expecting the worst almost automatically.

Here are two common ways our thoughts can be distorted:

"Half-empty" Thinking

Imagine a glass that is filled halfway. Would you say it is half empty or half full? Either statement is correct. However, focusing on the "half empty" part instead of the "half full" part can work against you. People who think this way are paying attention to only what's missing, bad, or wrong about a situation or person. If you do this, it becomes easier to miss what's good or hopeful about your situation.

Nicole had half-empty thinking when she only considered the times when her parents fought. Maybe there were times when her parents didn't fight, but she didn't acknowledge them. She also didn't consider the possibility that her parents could learn

Are Your Thoughts Getting in Your Way?

from their mistakes and do better. And she certainly didn't consider the good things that can result from talking with parents about problems, like a closer relationship or better understanding.

People can also think half-empty thoughts about themselves. For example, deep inside a person might be thinking, *I'm not smart. I never do well in school.* But that person may be leaving out something he or she is really good at, such as building or fixing things. When you've got a problem to solve, it's important to remember the things you do well. That way, you'll have more confidence about your ability to solve your problems.

Do you ignore the half-full part about your problems and focus too much on the half-empty part? Look back at the thoughts you noted in activity 6. Is there something positive or hopeful about your situation that you're not considering? A time when your problem wasn't a problem? Or, is there a positive characteristic about one or both of your parents or yourself that you're forgetting about? If so, write these positives below.

_____

_____

_____

_____

"Predicting the Worst" Thinking

"Predicting the worst" thinking is a little like "half-empty" thinking. The difference, though, is that predicting the worst takes the negative thought even further, and jumps to a firm, negative conclusion about the future.

These are two examples of predicting the worst: *If I talk to my parents about this problem, they will punish me for a month,* or *I'll make a fool out of myself if I try this solution, and my parents will laugh at me.*

Nicole's thoughts predicted the worst when she told herself, *No matter what I do, it won't change anything.*

When you're upset about your parents' separation or divorce, "predicting the worst" thoughts can seem completely true, even when they aren't.

Look back at the thoughts you noted in activity 6. Are you predicting the worst? If so, consider an opposite outcome. Write about it below.

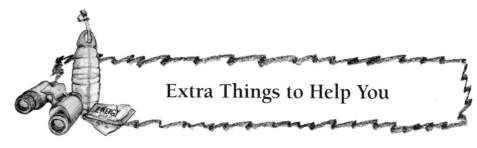

Extra Things to Help You

🐟 In activity 6, you identified the best solution to your problem. One way to help identify which solution really is best is asking yourself, how might my family feel about this solution (empathy builder)? Is this solution fair to them? Write your answers to these questions below.

🐟 If the problems resulting from your parents' separation or divorce get you so angry that you can't even think about solving them, jump ahead to chapter 7.

_____

_____

_____

_____

_____

_____

PRAYER

*Lord, my parents' separation or divorce has caused me some
problems. Sometimes I just try to ignore them, or keep
wishing that they will go away on their own.
The problems that are most difficult for me right now are
_____ and_____.
Show me what I can do to help solve them,
and fill me with hope that things can and will get better.
Be with me in everything, Lord, for you have the power
to bring good from every situation.
Help me to grow from this experience.
Amen.*

Take Aways

Write down two or three things in this chapter that you'd
like to remember or think will help you the most.

1.

2.

3.

Chapter Five

Divorce Solutions

How Do I Take Action?

Veejay's mom walked into the kitchen carrying several filled bags. "Can you help me with the groceries?" she asked him, then walked quickly back outside.

Veejay threw down his pencil. It always annoyed him to be interrupted when doing his homework. He got up and walked outside.

Mrs. Sandeep stood by the trunk of the car. She picked up three grocery bags. "I need you to take these in right away and put everything in the refrigerator," she said.

Veejay walked over to his mom without saying anything and took the bags. He was still mad at her for not letting him stay up later during school nights. He walked back to the kitchen and started putting the

items in the refrigerator. *One more order*, he thought.
It isn't fair at all.

After a few minutes, Mrs. Sandeep walked back
in with the rest of the groceries. "Thanks, Veejay," she
said.

Veejay was angry, but continued putting away the
groceries.

"What would you like for dinner?" Veejay's mom asked. "There are leftovers . . . or we could have samosas."

"It doesn't matter," Veejay said. *I'd rather she gave me a choice about my bedtime like Dad does*, he thought.

"Let's have samosas then. Aren't they still your favorite?" Veejay's mom asked. "I'll have the leftovers tomorrow for lunch." She took out a frying pan from the cabinet by the stove, then got the ground meat from the refrigerator.

She acts as if going to bed at 8:30 is no big deal, Veejay thought. *None of my friends have to go to bed that early.* His heart pounded harder against his chest. He felt as if his whole body was on fire.

"You're always giving me orders!" Veejay suddenly blurted out.

"Excuse me?" Mrs. Sandeep said.

"I'm sick of it. All you care about is what you want, not what I want."

"Are you talking about your bedtime?" his mom asked.

Veejay stormed out of the kitchen.

"Veejay, this conversation will have to wait until after dinner," she called after him.

Later that night, after Veejay finished his homework, he looked at a handout that his school counselor had given him about how to communicate with parents. He didn't want to admit it, but looking over the tips Veejay realized he had made some mistakes—maybe more than a few.

It was 8:25. Frustrated, Veejay shoved the handout back in his backpack and turned out the light. But he couldn't fall asleep. Part of him wanted to talk to his mom about his bedtime, but another part wanted to forget about her and just find a way that he could live with his dad for good. Veejay lay quietly in bed thinking. He even asked God what to do. A few moments later, Veejay realized something. *My mom will always be my mom, no matter what,* he thought. *It's not right for me to push her out of my life just because I'm upset about something.*

Veejay got out of bed. He took a deep breath and walked down the hallway to his mother's bedroom. The door was open. She was sitting in a chair, reading a book.

"Mom?" Veejay said softly. "Are you busy right now?"

"No," she said and put down her book. "What's on your mind?"

"I can't sleep," Veejay said.

"What's wrong, Veejay?" she asked.

"It's about my bedtime," Veejay said. "I want you to hear me out on this."

"Okay," his mom said.

Veejay sat down on her bed. "The reason I'd like to stay up later is because, after doing my homework and chores, there's hardly any time left over for things I want to do."

His mom nodded, as if she understood.

"And, when I go to bed at 8:30, I end up staying up till 9 anyway, because I can't fall asleep that early. So, it's like I'm wasting that time. And Mom, nobody else at school goes to bed that early anymore."

"Hmm, I didn't realize that," Veejay's mom said. "How about we try the later bedtime and see how it works out? I guess as long as you get up in the morning . . ."

"Really?" Veejay interrupted with excitement. "That'd be great!" He looked at the clock on his mom's nightstand. "That means I have fifteen more minutes. What's the book you're reading?"

Veejay and his mom talked about the book, then Veejay went to bed and slept soundly. He and his mom started a ritual of talking every night before Veejay went to bed. He looked forward to having that time with his mom. He also felt better knowing that he could do something to solve some of the problems he had since his parents' divorce.

Communication Benefits

Veejay was reluctant to talk with his mom because he doubted it would make a difference.

Below are some benefits of talking constructively with your parents about the problems you face because of their separation or divorce.

Check any that you might need to remember.

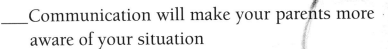

___Communication will make your parents more aware of your situation

Parents are not mind readers. Remember, too, that the separation or divorce is not easy for them either. As a result, they can become more focused on their own problems and forget what you may be going through.

___Communication can prevent your anger from building

Have you ever gotten so angry that you talked back to your parent like Veejay did? Or maybe you did something else that got you in trouble? If you don't try to work out the problems you have by talking with your parents, it's more likely that your anger will build up and cause you to blow up later.

___Communication can strengthen your relationship with your parents

When you communicate in positive ways with your parents, you build trust and respect in your relationship with them. Spending more time talking things over can also help you get to know one another better, too.

___You will be practicing communication skills that will help you in other ways

Knowing how to communicate well will help you succeed in other areas of your life. Practicing those skills now will help to deepen your friendships, improve your relationships with teachers, and help you do better quality work in school. Later, these same skills will be helpful in your work and home life.

___You will grow spiritually

Another benefit of communicating better with parents is that it can help you grow spiritually. That happens when you ask the Holy Spirit to guide you, and then letting him do just that.

___Relying on the Holy Spirit

When you were baptized, you received grace from the Holy Spirit. This grace can be seen in the Holy Spirit's seven gifts. They are:

Gifts of the Holy Spirit

Wisdom—the ability to see things from God's point of view

Understanding—insight into the truths of our faith and what they mean for us

Counsel (right judgment)—the openness to both seek and give good advice when there is a decision to be made

Fortitude (courage)—the strength to do what is right even when it's difficult

Knowledge—knowing God in a personal way

Piety (reverence)—which leads us to prayer and enables us to love and worship God

Fear of the Lord (wonder and awe)—which helps us to recognize, respect, and wonder at God's unique power and holiness

When you receive the sacrament of Confirmation, these gifts are strengthened even more. When you cooperate with the Holy Spirit and use the gifts he has given you, your relationship with God will be like a seed that grows and bears fruit. St. Paul wrote that "the fruit of the Holy Spirit is love, joy, peace, patience, kindness, generosity, faithfulness, gentleness, and self-control" (Galatians 5:22). The world would be a much better place if we all had more of those!

Gifts and Fruit of the Holy Spirit

Veejay was upset about the different rules of his parents, especially his mom's rule about his bedtime.

He got so mad that he was tempted to push her out of his life.

Instead, though, he asked God to help him, and drew on the gifts he had already been given.

Which *gifts* of the Holy Spirit (see page 87) helped Veejay in this situation? Write them below.

_____

_____

The Holy Spirit helped Veejay make a choice to do what was right.

Talking with his mom produced some of what St. Paul called the fruit of the Holy Spirit.

Write down one (or more) of the *fruits* (named on the opposite page) that developed as a result below. Explain.

_____

_____

_____

_____

_____

Gifts and Fruit
of the Holy Spirit in Your Life

Consider a problem you're having with your parents' separation or divorce.

Which of the Holy Spirit's *gifts* could help you?

Write down one (or more) of these gifts below. Next, explain your answer.

_____

_____

_____

What *fruit* of the Holy Spirit could develop in you as a result?

Write down one (or more) of those fruits below. Explain your answer.

_____

_____

_____

_____

_____

_____

_____

Communication Dos and Don'ts

In order to communicate well, it's important to know some dos and don'ts. Like learning to play a sport, part of learning how to communicate well depends on understanding the rules and knowing the boundaries. Do you know the rules and boundaries for good communication? Test your knowledge by answering the questions that follow.

Communication Out-of-Bounds

Veejay made some mistakes in communicating with his mother.

What do you think they were?

_____

_____

(Check the next section, Communication Rules, if you need help.)

Communication Scores

Veejay also made some very good choices in communicating with his mom.

What do you think those were?

_____

_____

(Check the next section, Communication Rules, if you need help.)

Communication Rules

Now, it's your turn. Look over the rules below. Then, check off whether or not you follow them.

▼.▼.▼. Choose one problem to focus on

Do you have more than one problem that you want to discuss with one or both of your parents? If so, you may find it hard to resist bringing up all of them at once. If you do, though, your parents are likely to feel overwhelmed, and you may give them the impression that you're demanding too much. As a result, you may not make any progress at all.

Instead, decide which problem is most important to you, and focus only on it.

_____I stay within this boundary.

_____I often go out-of-bounds on this rule.

▼.▼.▼. Figure out what is most important to you

If you figure out beforehand what you really hope to achieve, you'll have a better chance of accomplishing it.

Your parents probably want you to be happy, but they can't read your mind. The more you can help them understand what is important to you, the more likely your parents will consider it. For example, do you want your parent's advice, or their permission to do something? Maybe you just want them to listen. Figure this out beforehand, then tell them what is important to you, and ask for time to talk about it. Here are some examples:

"Mom, I'd like to get your permission to visit Dad over the holidays. Can we talk about what I'd like to do?"

"Dad, I'd like it if you and I can do things just ourselves sometimes, without bringing your girlfriend along. Can we talk about this?"

"Mom, can I talk to you? I need your advice about something."

_____I stay within this boundary.

_____I often go out-of-bounds on this rule.

♥.♥. Pick a good time to talk

Choosing a good time is important, especially since talking about a problem can be stressful for everyone. One way to increase your chances of having the conversation go smoothly is to pick a time that works for both you and your parent. For example, if you're upset, wait until you have calmed down. Otherwise, your emotions might easily get the best of you. It's the same with your parents. Make sure they're not busy with something else, or overly tired.

If you're not sure whether it's a good time for your parent to talk, just ask, "Can we talk? Is now a good time?" Or, if it seems like there's never a good time for your parent, say, "I need to talk with you. When is a good time?" Your parent will appreciate your consideration.

_____I stay within this boundary.

_____I often go out-of-bounds on this rule.

There are also important rules to remember once you start the conversation:

During the Conversation

▼.▼.▼. Keep a good attitude

Just as unexpected things can happen when playing a sport, unexpected obstacles can turn up during a conversation. For example, maybe your dad gets interrupted by an important phone call, or your mom becomes upset about something you bring up. It's important to stay positive and continue to cooperate with them. A good way to show this is with a good attitude. This means being understanding and patient, and using a respectful tone of voice.

_____I stay within this boundary.

_____I often go out-of-bounds on this rule.

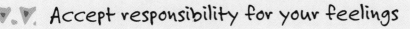

▼.▼. Accept responsibility for your feelings

It can be easy to blame your parents for problems you're experiencing as a result of their separation or divorce. However, that won't help you, and in fact, it often makes a problem even worse. Here's why: First, when you blame someone else for how you feel, you're actually saying that you have no power to help yourself. Believing that there is nothing you can do will only keep you stuck in your crummy feelings. It will also keep you stuck in the situation you'd like to change. There is almost always something you can do to make a bad situation better. Second, blaming others is a sign that you are unwilling to accept any responsibility or work together to solve a problem. This attitude will discourage your parent from working with you to find a solution.

_____I stay within this boundary.

_____I often go out-of-bounds on this rule.

▼.▼. Be as truthful and fair as you can

If you are truthful and fair when discussing a problem, your parent is likely to listen seriously to what you say and not feel the need to correct you. The self-control that honesty and fairness require also shows that you're trying your best to work out a solution and not just blowing off steam.

A good way to show that you're being truthful and fair when you speak with your parent is to give specific examples. For instance, suppose you feel left out whenever your dad's girlfriend is around. Which of these statements do you think would help you communicate more clearly?

1) "Dad, the last time we went to the movies with Mindy, I felt left out because no one asked what movie I wanted to see."

OR

2) "Dad, I always feel left out whenever Mindy is around."

The answer is statement 1 because it gives a specific example of the problem you are trying to solve. While statement 2 may describe how you feel, it doesn't really help you find a solution. Statements that are too general can turn a discussion into a debate, or leave your parent feeling like what you're saying came out of nowhere.

A good way to stay truthful and fair is to avoid using words like "always" and "never."

_____I stay within this boundary.

_____I often go out-of-bounds on this rule.

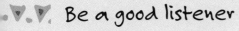

Be a good listener

Because a good conversation goes two ways, listening will also help you communicate well. How can you be a good listener?

Give your mom or dad a chance to talk, and wait until your parent finishes before you talk again.

Pay attention to everything your parent says.

Minimize distractions. This means putting down your book, turning off the TV, pausing your video game, or stopping anything else that may prevent you from listening fully to your parent.

Give small verbal responses as your parent talks. Here are some examples: "Uh-huh," "Sure," "I hear you," "Really?"

Ask questions if you don't understand something.

_____I stay within this boundary.

_____I often go out-of-bounds on this rule.

♥.♥.♥. Use good body language

You may not be aware of this but, in a conversation, your body also talks! This is called nonverbal communication, and it can "speak" louder than your words. Using good body language is an important part of communicating well. Here are some examples of good body language:

Making eye contact (looking your parent in the eye)

Moving closer to your parent (but not too close)

Turning toward your parent (not away from him or her)

Sitting up straight (not slouching in a chair)

Nodding from time to time when your parent is talking

Smiling or having a friendly and cooperative look on your face (not a frown, smirk, or angry look)

Keeping your arms in a relaxed position in front of you (not crossing them)

If you use good body language, your parent is likely to feel more relaxed and more willing to consider what you are saying.

_____I stay within this boundary.

_____I often go out-of-bounds on this rule.

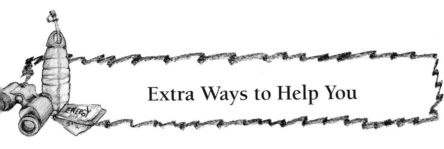

Extra Ways to Help You

Read about the saints and their good works

Do the problems related to your parents' divorce seem impossible to solve? If so, learning about the lives of some saints might inspire you. There are lots of books about the saints that have been written just for kids.

Saint Jude and Saint Rita both showed incredible perseverance throughout their lives. Saint Joseph, the patron saint of families and fathers, is also the unofficial patron saint against doubt and hesitation. And Saint Therese of Lisieux, known as the Little Flower, learned how to offer up little sacrifices with love.

Try to talk with one or both of your parents every day about everyday things

Try to talk often with your parents about less sensitive topics, such as how your team did, what happened at school, or what's for dinner. This will make it easier to talk with your mom or dad about more serious stuff when you need to.

PRAYER

*Lord, it can be hard to say what I need to say in a way
my parents can hear it. Sometimes I'm afraid to tell them
what's bothering me. Other times, I let my feelings get
the best of me and act disrespectfully. Lord, help me
to be patient with others and myself.*

*Give me the strength to keep a positive attitude,
and the grace to cooperate with your Holy Spirit.
You have the power to bring good from every situation.
Help me to grow from this experience. Amen.*

Take Aways

Write down two or three things in this chapter that you'd
like to remember or think will help you the most.

1.

2.

3.

Chapter Six

Caught Between

How Do I Get Out of the Middle?

It was Saturday morning. Maria quickly put on her robe and walked into the kitchen. Her mom was seated at the table reading the newspaper.

"Good morning, Mom," Maria said, giving her a big smile.

"Good morning," her mom said, putting down the newspaper. "Did you get a good night's sleep?"

Maria nodded, even though she hadn't slept well at all. She was usually so excited to visit her mom on the weekends that it kept her up most of the night. Ever since her parents divorced five years ago, Maria saw her mom only every other weekend and, sometimes, during holidays and the summer.

As Maria and her mom ate breakfast, they talked about Maria's school and friends. Then, her mom talked about her new job and some of her co-workers. The morning was going perfectly until her mom changed the subject and started talking about Maria's father.

"You were too young to remember," Maria's mom said, "but, when your grandmother was alive, your father and his siblings wouldn't even sit with her at the holidays when dinner was served. They hardly ever talked with her, either. And it was all because she danced with another man at a wedding."

Maria didn't know what to say, so she said nothing. Her mom continued, but Maria's thoughts soon drifted off. *Why is Mom telling me this?* she wondered. *Is it because Mom sometimes danced with other men too? It's strange,* Maria told herself. *It's like hearing a secret from one of my friends.*

"I felt bad for her," Maria's mom continued. "So, I visited with her whenever I was home from college. I think she looked forward to that. I never judged her, like your father and his siblings did."

Maria looked down at the table, then out the window. She wasn't sure how she felt about the conversation. On one hand, Maria liked hearing her mom talk about personal things because it made her feel close to her. But on the other hand, Maria was very uncomfortable hearing it. The more she listened to her mom's story, the angrier she got. It was like her mom was, once again, pressuring Maria to take sides in the divorce.

After breakfast, when Maria was getting dressed, she thought more about what her mom had told her. She figured her mom was probably telling the truth. *But there are always two sides to every story*, she thought, remembering what her favorite teacher had said once. *Plus, that information has nothing to do with me. Shouldn't Mom just let it go?*

Maria's teacher had also taught them about the importance of trusting their instincts when talking to strangers. *Even though Mom isn't a stranger*, Maria thought, *it still seems wrong for her to be sharing this old story with me.*

Maria hoped her mom wouldn't tell her any more stories like this one. It made Maria feel like she had been placed in the middle of a game of tug-of-war. If it happened again, she decided, she would definitely change the subject.

Tug-of-War Situations

Maria felt put in the middle by the story her mom told her.

Below are some ways that parents can put kids in the middle of a conflict.

Check off any that describe what either or both of your parents do.

___Tell me too much about divorce problems

___Tell me bad things about my other parent (or say them when I'm in the room and can hear them)

___Ask me to report on what my other parent says or does

___Fight in front of me

___Tell me to ask or tell my other parent something important (instead of my parent doing this him/herself)

___Force me to choose sides (for example, saying "If you want me to go to your game, don't invite your father; otherwise I won't go.")

___Other. Please describe here: _____

_____

How the Tug-of-War Affects Me

Maria got angry with her mom because what she said put Maria in the middle.

Choose one situation that you checked in activity 1.

Describe or draw your thoughts and/or feelings about it.

Tug-of-War Solutions

Maria didn't know what to do when her mom put her in the middle.
So, she just listened.

Choose one situation that you checked in activity 1.

Describe or draw how you handle it.

4 Solution Outcomes

Maria's solution had positive and negative consequences, or outcomes.

What are the positive and negative outcomes of your solution?

Use what you drew or wrote for activity 3 and complete the chart below to find out.

Example

Maria's Tug-of-War Problem: My mom tells me bad things about my dad

Tug-of-War Solution	Positive Outcome	Negative Outcome
Say and do nothing	I sometimes feel close to Mom because she is sharing private information with me	I end up feeling uncomfortable, angry, and put in the middle

My Tug-of-War Problem: _____

_____

Tug-of-War Solution	Positive Outcome	Negative Outcome

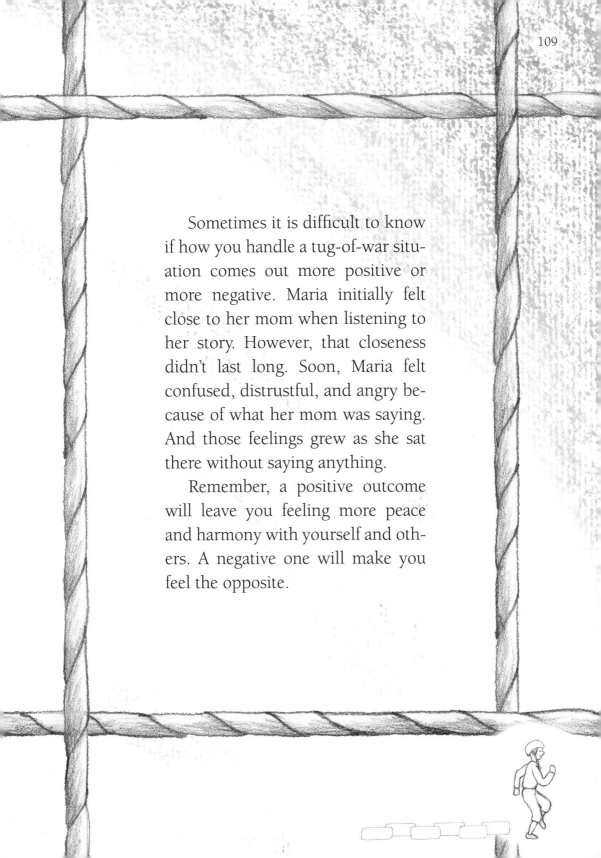

Sometimes it is difficult to know if how you handle a tug-of-war situation comes out more positive or more negative. Maria initially felt close to her mom when listening to her story. However, that closeness didn't last long. Soon, Maria felt confused, distrustful, and angry because of what her mom was saying. And those feelings grew as she sat there without saying anything.

Remember, a positive outcome will leave you feeling more peace and harmony with yourself and others. A negative one will make you feel the opposite.

Solution Evaluation

Maria's solution had more of a negative outcome than a positive one.

Look back at your answer in activity 4. Which of your outcomes is more positive?

Explain your answer below.

_____

_____

_____

_____

So, how can you make your outcome more positive than negative? If you're like most kids, you may feel afraid to do something about an uncomfortable situation and, as a result, do nothing. However, it's important to try to get out of the middle if you're there. Doing something positive will also help you to avoid being put in the middle again.

Usually, it's best to start by speaking up. This means expressing to your parent how you feel about being put in the middle, or asking him or her to stop doing what puts you there. You can do this either verbally in a conversation, or by writing a note or letter.

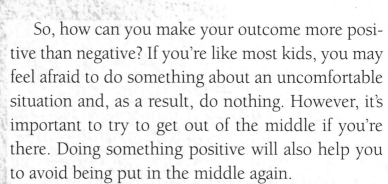

Speak Up

While speaking up for yourself can be hard to do, it's an important way of doing your part to help solve a problem. Speaking up can help your parent too. Often parents aren't even aware that something they are saying or doing is putting you in the middle.

Consider Maria's mother. Although she didn't mean to do anything wrong, it was inappropriate for her to tell Maria a story from the past. Like most parents, though, Maria's mother probably didn't think that sharing the story would hurt Maria. This was mostly because she still was angry with Maria's father. That anger made it harder for Maria's mom to exercise good judgment and resist telling Maria something negative about her dad and his family.

If Maria had spoken up and told her mom how the story was affecting her or that repeating it was wrong, her mother may have stopped. As a result, Maria would have helped her mom behave in a healthier way, a way that's also more pleasing to God.

Another reason why it's important to speak up is because all our relationships are best when they have healthy boundaries.

Healthy Boundaries

A boundary is like a dividing line or limit. It shows where something ends and something else begins. For example, consider your room. This is a specific area in your home that belongs to you, or you and a sibling if you share a room. You probably decorate it (or part of it) in a way that you like, and you are responsible for cleaning it (or part of it) too. Your mom or dad has another room. Are you responsible for cleaning their room by doing things like hanging up their clothes and making their bed, when this is not one of your assigned chores? No. Are they responsible for cleaning your room? No.

Sometimes, though, a parent can forget this and expect you to clean up their room. It may not mean physical cleaning like dusting or vacuuming; it could mean expecting you to take on other responsibilities that do not belong to you. When this happens, a parent is disrespecting your boundaries. Here are some examples of how parents might do this:

- By telling you details about personal problems because your parent needs emotional support

- By asking you for advice on adult matters (for example, which job to take or whom they should date)

- By expecting you to take care of them (for example, not wanting you to go out with friends so you can stay home and keep that parent company)

- By asking you to report on what your other parent says or does (see activity 1)

- By having you ask or tell your other parent something important, when your parent should be doing this (see activity 1)

A parent can also disrespect your boundaries if he or she tries to "clean up your room" or, in other words, do for you what you can and should be doing yourself. Here again, this doesn't mean cleaning in a physical way, but in an emotional way. This type of parent does not respect your personal freedom and privacy. Here are some examples:

- A parent who tries to control all of your decisions

- A parent who tries to manipulate you with guilt trips or threats

- A parent who does not respect your feelings

- A parent who does not respect your privacy

If you find yourself in any of these situations, you can take steps to set healthy boundaries. When you do, it shows that you regard your feelings and values as important. Treating yourself with respect makes you stronger. It also encourages others—including your parents—to respect you more.

Setting healthy boundaries with your parents can also benefit them. They may, understandably, be very stressed or upset about the breakup, just as you are. This overload can cause them to say or do things that they do not realize are hurtful at the time. By setting a healthy boundary you may, in fact, help and inspire them to do the same. The beauty of all this is that your relationship with your parent may become stronger in the process.

How to Set Healthy Boundaries

Learning how to set healthy boundaries can be difficult, especially if your parents haven't set a good example for you. If this describes your parents, think of someone else who would be a good role model for you, like a grandparent, an aunt or uncle, a teacher or coach, or a priest, deacon, nun, or other member of your parish staff. This person would be someone who does the following:

Lets others know, in a clear and firm way, when their behavior is unacceptable

Sets limits with everyone and in a consistent way

Respects the belongings of others

Says no when necessary

Is confident about expressing a point of view, but also lets others express theirs

Think of this person now and write his or her name here:

_____

Watch how this person sets boundaries and try to imitate his or her example in your own life.

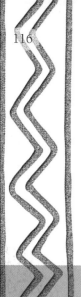

Speaking up and setting boundaries isn't easy, and you may need to try over and over before getting it right. It can help to have someone work with you. So when you think you're ready to set boundaries with your parents, think about asking a trustworthy adult, like your school counselor, to coach you through the process.

Remembering these tips can help, too.

Trust Your Instincts

An instinct is a hunch or gut feeling. When Maria trusted her instincts, she got a better understanding that her mother was doing something wrong.

Remember, if your parent is doing something that seems wrong or makes you uncomfortable, it is likely to be wrong, and you probably need to address it. Pay attention to these feelings.

Think About What God Wants for You

One way to evaluate if your parent may be disrespecting healthy boundaries is to think about what God would want for you in this situation. God loves you more than anyone else does or ever will. He wants all of us to treat both others and ourselves with respect. Respecting yourself will help you grow toward independence.

Include Your Feelings as Part of the Conversation

It can be awkward to set boundaries with parents, especially since it's our parents (and other adults) who usually set boundaries or limits with us. Like most kids, you may feel nervous about communicating boundaries and, as a result, say nothing. But don't let those fears win out! Instead, include them in your talk with your parent. For example, you could say, "Mom, I need to talk with you about something, but I'm afraid it will make you angry."

If you do try to have this conversation, remember to use a responsibility statement. A responsibility statement is a way of communicating that you are taking responsibility for your feelings and co-operating in solving a problem. It has three parts: "I feel," "when you," and "because." You can develop a responsibility statement by completing the blanks in the following sentence:

I feel _____ (try to be specific about how you feel about this boundary situation) when you _____
(describe what your parent does or has done that you believe disrespects your boundaries) because _____ (include the reason why you think you feel this way).

Explain What You Don't Like and Ask Your Parent to Stop

Explain to your parent what he or she said or did that put you in the middle or made you uncomfortable, and ask him or her to stop. For example, Maria could have said, "Mom, I love you and Dad and want you both in my life. But when you tell me about mean things Dad has done, I feel like you're trying to make me choose between you. That isn't fair, and I'd like you to stop."

Consider Writing Your Parent a Note

If it's too scary to talk with your parent face-to-face, write a note to him or her about the tug-of-war situation. This can make it easier to focus more on what you need to say and less about how it might upset your parent. Here, too, remember to use a responsibility statement.

Back Up Your Words with Actions

You've probably heard the saying, "actions speak louder than words." If you speak up and your parent doesn't try to change or doesn't take you seriously, back up your words with actions. For example, if you ask your parents to stop fighting in front of you and they don't, consider leaving the room the next time it happens. Or, if you're talking on the phone and your dad starts telling you unpleasant things about your mom, consider telling your dad that you need to end the call.

6 Direct and in the Open

Maria decided that she would change the subject, if her mom told her another inappropriate story in the future.

However, that strategy might not work, because it's too indirect.

It also doesn't nurture understanding and respect in Maria's relationship with her mother.

Write what you could say to your parent that may help you from being put in the middle.

(Look back at the tips if you need help.)

_____

_____

_____

_____

_____

_____

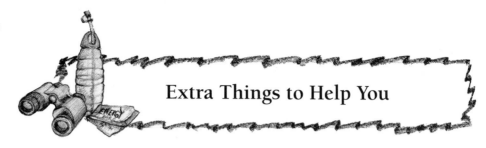

Extra Things to Help You

Is there another student in your class who is bothering you in some way? Or do you have a sibling or cousin who is? If so, practice speaking up and setting boundaries with him or her. This could help you when you set boundaries with your parents or other adults in your life.

Try to look at your situation from your parents' side. Imagine what your parents might be feeling that causes them to act this way. Is it guilt, hurt, or fear? Trying to stand in your parents' shoes can help you take their actions less personally. This is possible when you begin to see that your parents' actions are about who they are, and not about who you are (empathy builder).

If boundary problems are something you face on a regular basis, consider sharing this chapter with your parents. It may help them help themselves as well as you.

PRAYER

*Lord, my family is stressed, and I'm not always sure
how to stay out of the middle. Give me the courage to set
healthy boundaries with my parents when necessary.
Guide my parents, Lord, and help me to remember that
they still love me. Show me how to make choices that
keep me out of the middle, but are also respectful to others.
Teach us all how to find peace even when we feel upset.
You have the power to bring good from every situation.
Help me to grow from this experience.*
Amen.

Take Aways

Write down two or three things in this chapter that you'd
like to remember or think will help you the most.

1.

2.

3.

Chapter Seven

Anger

How Do I Handle It?

Zach walked into the family room. He frowned and sighed loudly when he saw his sister Alexis seated at the game table, doing homework. He wished he could be alone, but the family room was the only place in their new house that had a TV. Zach turned it on and plopped down in the lounge chair. *This place is so small,* he thought, *it's like a hotel room. I can't get any privacy anywhere.* His mom had promised to get him a TV for his room, but then his parents divorced, and she said they didn't have the money. *What else won't they have the money for?* he wondered. *Will I have to stop going to Saint Raphael's next and leave all my friends? Or quit karate class?* Zach felt his head start to pound. He tried to ignore it and turned up the volume with the remote control.

"Could you please turn the TV down?" Alexis asked. "I'm trying to finish my report for social studies."

"Your homework is so easy," Zach said, wanting to make her feel bad. "You must be really dumb if you can't finish it during school."

"What's really dumb is that show you're watching," Alexis replied.

Zach mimicked his sister, "What's really dumb is that show you're watching."

"Could you *please* turn down the volume a little?" Alexis repeated. "I'm trying to concentrate."

"No, go somewhere else if it bothers you," Zach said without looking at her.

"There are still boxes everywhere," Alexis said. "I can't go anywhere else."

Zach felt a rush of energy rise in him. "That's your problem and Mom's. She's another dumb one for making us move into this place."

Alexis got up and walked over to him. Planting her hands on her hips, she said, "Mom didn't have a choice. Dad was the one who filed for divorce. And she has a lot more bills now, because of it. She's just trying to save money."

Zach didn't like being lectured to, especially by his younger sister. He felt his face get hot.

"You could at least do your chores," Alexis added.

"Shut up, pea brain," Zach said, and he threw a pillow at her.

Alexis stormed back to the game table, put her worksheets and notebook in her backpack, and headed toward the door. Before leaving the family room, she turned to Zach and said, "You're acting just like Dad."

Zach shot up from his seat and charged toward Alexis. She ran down the hall to her room and slammed the door. "I told you to shut up, pea brain!" Zach shouted. He headed back to the family room and sat back down. Then he turned up the volume on the TV as loud as it would go.

What Gets You Angry?

Zach was angry about moving into a smaller house and not getting a TV for his room.

Is there anything that has happened since your parents' separation or divorce that makes you angry?

If so, write or draw a picture below about what angers you.

Like excitement or disappointment, anger is a normal human emotion. People get angry about all kinds of things. But when their parents separate or divorce, lots of kids experience anger more frequently, and sometimes more strongly, than they are used to. Often, that anger covers up other feelings. Since hurt, worry, or frustration can be more painful and overwhelming to feel, it's not unusual to express them with anger instead. It's also easy to make the mistake of thinking that it is more "grown-up" or "strong" to be angry than it is to express other feelings that might make us feel weak or as if we're not in control.

Feelings Underneath Anger

Zach was worried about money. In addition to not getting a TV for his room, he wondered whether he'd have to change schools or quit karate.

Look back at your answer to activity 1.

What feelings might be underneath the anger you described?

Consider emotions like worry, fear, sadness, hurt, embarrassment, jealousy, confusion, and disappointment.

Write or draw a picture below about one of these feelings.

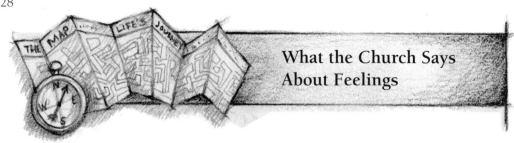

What the Church Says About Feelings

Emotions are not right or wrong. It's not wrong to feel angry, just like it's not wrong to feel happy. What can be wrong, though, is what you choose to do with your anger. Anger is especially hard to handle in a positive way because it is such a strong emotion. If being angry causes you to seek revenge, become judgmental, or say or do things that hurt others, then your anger has caused you to sin.

This teaching, however, doesn't mean you should allow yourself to be bullied or treated disrespectfully. There may even be times in which it is necessary—and right—to defend yourself. However, Jesus wants you to do everything you can to avoid hurting others in the process.

Why is it important to take proper care of anger? Because otherwise it can grow to the point where it becomes extreme or out of control. That kind of anger, called wrath, becomes like poison in the person who is angry. Wrath is one of the seven capital sins. They are called "capital," or serious, because they can be the source of other sins (*Catechism of the Catholic Church*, section 1866).

How to Control Anger Before It Controls You

We know how important it is to pay attention to when a traffic light changes from green to yellow, or from yellow to red. Suppose you're riding your bike toward a busy intersection. If you don't pay attention to the traffic light, you won't see it change. As a result, you may cross the street when you're not supposed to, and you may get hurt.

In order to handle anger in a good, positive, and healthy way, you'll need to pay attention to your anger warning signs. These are signs in your body that tell you when you're getting angry. Recognizing them will help you prevent your reaction to anger from turning a bad situation into a worse one.

Anger Warning Signs

Zach had several warning signs that he was becoming angry enough to lose control.

His head started pounding. He wanted to make his sister feel bad. He felt a rush of energy, and his face got hot.

What are your anger warning signs? Check off all of them below.

____Head pounds

____Heart rate increases

____Feel hot in my face or neck

____Grind my teeth

____Clench my jaw

____Get a headache

____Get a stomach ache

____Get knots in my stomach

____Get sweaty palms

____Shake or tremble

____Feel dizzy

____Feel a rush of energy

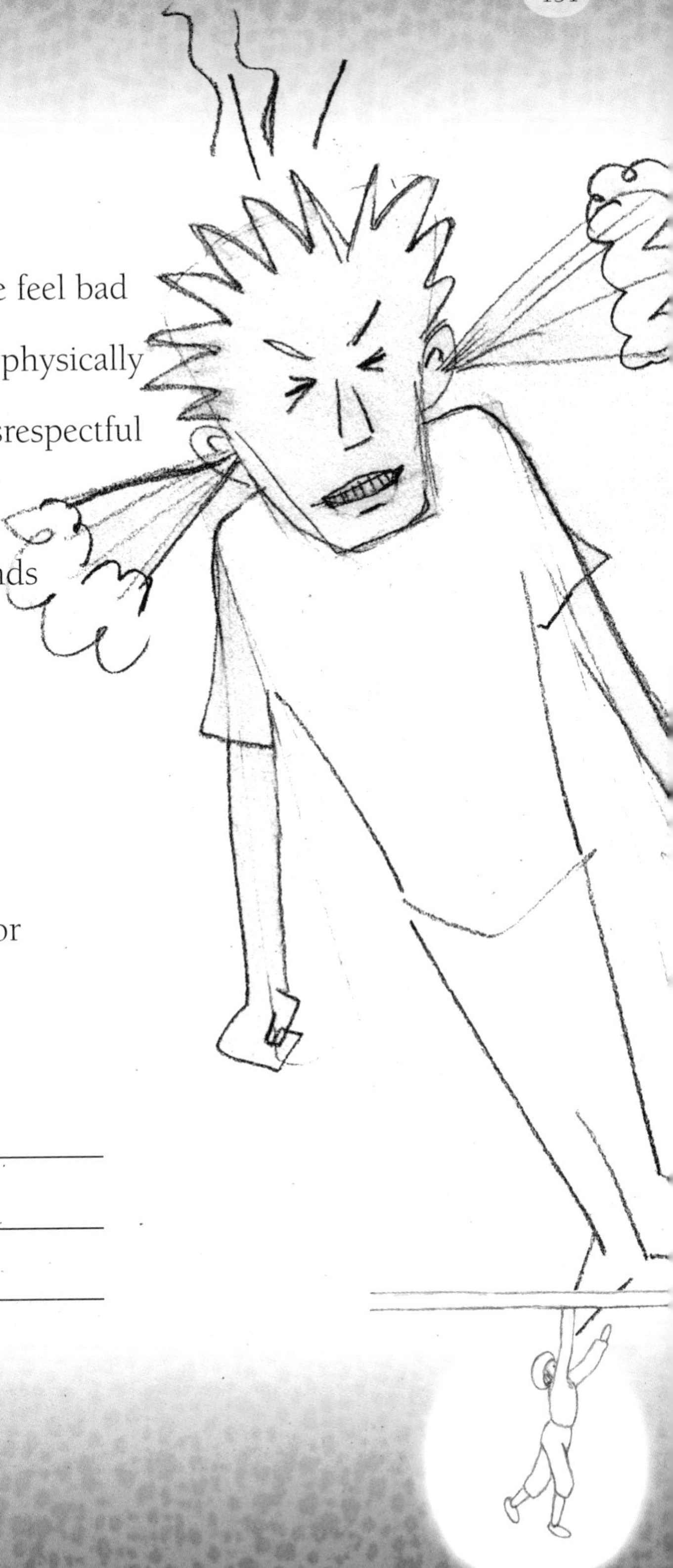

_____Want to make someone feel bad

_____Want to hurt someone physically

_____Start being mean or disrespectful

_____Rub my head

_____Form fists with my hands

_____Feel like screaming

_____Start to pace

_____Raise my voice

_____Get sarcastic

_____Lose my sense of humor

_____Cry

_____Other. Please describe:

_____

_____

_____

4

How Do You Express Anger?

Zach ignored his anger warning signs. This caused him to treat his sister unkindly.

Do you ignore your anger warning signs too?

On the next page check off what you usually do when feeling angry.

If what you do isn't listed, write it here:

_____

_____

_____

_____

_____

_____

_____

_____I keep anger inside or ignore it

_____Hit or kick the person

_____Call him/her a name back

_____Threaten him/her

_____Tease or insult others

_____Talk back to others

_____Plan a nasty prank

_____Spread a nasty rumor

_____Go somewhere unsafe

_____Eat too much or too little

_____Hurt myself physically

_____Hurt an animal

_____Destroy other's belongings/property

_____Tell yourself positive thoughts to calm down (such as, "I can handle this.")

_____Stop and think about the consequences if you take anger out on someone else

_____Take 3 deep breaths and/or count backward slowly

_____Talk it out with a friend or adult

_____Write it out

_____Scream into a pillow

_____Punch a pillow or punching bag

_____Rip up old newspapers or magazines, then crumble them up

_____Exercise or play a sport

_____Do something creative

_____Listen to relaxing music

_____Read

_____Pray or talk with God

5. Anger Grade

Count the number of check marks you made in activity 4 and note them below.

_____ Checks in left column

_____ Checks in right column

| The checks in the left column describe negative ways to express anger. | The checks in the right column describe positive ways to express anger. |

Based on your number of check marks, what grade would you give yourself for how well you're noticing your anger warning signs and expressing anger?

Explain your answer

_____

_____

_____

_____

If what you do wasn't listed, decide whether it belongs in the left or right column.

Now that you have a better understanding of positive and negative ways to express anger, it's time to create an action plan.

6 Your Anger Plan ● ● ● ● ● ● ● ● ● ● ● ●

Write down at least 3 things you will try
(or continue to do) when feeling angry.

1. _____

_____

2. _____

_____

3. _____

_____

If you need help, look back at
the right column of activity 4.

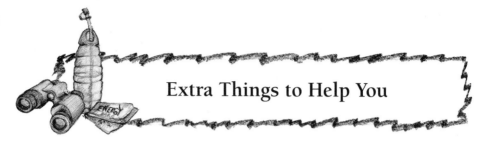

🐥 Pay extra attention to your anger for the next week or two weeks. Keep a log by writing down any warning signs you experience. After you have several entries, look back at your log to see if you experienced any of the signs more than once. If so, circle or highlight these signs.

🐌 Think of a person you admire for the way he or she handles anger. If possible, ask this person how he or she developed this strength.

☀ Are you so angry at your parents for the separation or divorce that you are trying to punish them in some way? Sometimes, kids try to do this by not speaking to a parent, getting into trouble, or not doing their homework. If this describes you, try these steps:

1) Get your anger out by writing one or both of your parents a letter about how you feel. This is a letter "for your eyes only," where you can say everything and anything you want to say without worry about how it may make others feel. You must rip up or shred the letter once you're done writing it, though.

2) Take a step back from your anger and ask, "Am I hurting myself by what I'm doing?" Consider things like not doing your best in school or choosing to do things you know are wrong. If this describes you, write a more detailed answer to this question on a separate sheet of paper. Keep it in a place where you can quickly refer to it when needed.

3) Realize that two wrongs don't make a right. It's also important to remember that anger can cause us to lose fairness and understanding. As a result, you may be making an incorrect assumption about your parent. We never know what's in a person's heart; only God does.

4) Ask God to help you understand your parent better. This can lessen your anger and also help you take steps to forgive your parent.

PRAYER

*Lord, I'm angry, and sometimes I don't even know
how angry I am. Help me to recognize it before
I lose control. Show me how to calm myself down.
Give me the strength to handle my anger in positive ways,
and the courage to see and feel the hurt that lies beneath
my anger. Lord, give me the gift of empathy so I can better
understand the people I'm angry with and be able to forgive
them. You have the power to bring good from every
situation. Help me to grow from this experience.
Amen.*

Take Aways

Write down two or three things in this chapter that you'd
like to remember or think will help you the most.

1.

2.

3.

Chapter Eight

God

Does He Care?

It was three o'clock. The last school bell rang. The students in Mrs. Connor's classroom lined up and faced the crucifix for the after-school prayers. But Michael stayed in his seat and stared down at his desk. He felt sad. He was thinking about summer vacation and all the fun things he did with his dad. After Michael's parents divorced, his dad moved so far away that Michael had to fly in an airplane to visit him. Now Michael saw his dad only in the summer and at Christmas.

A student spoke over the loudspeaker and led everyone in prayer. She thanked God for the many gifts God gave them. Then, during the prayer, she asked for forgiveness for the times they ignored God's will.

Michael crunched his eyebrows. He didn't understand what God's will was for him. *If I had my way,* he
thought, *my dad would live a whole lot closer.*

Mrs. Connor walked over to Michael. "Michael,
please join the other students," she said. But Michael
turned his back to her and looked down at the floor.
It's not fair, he thought. *My dad should be at my Scout
meetings like the other dads.*

The class said a closing prayer together, then made
the sign of the cross. Michael held his arms tight.

As the other students gathered their backpacks
and began to leave the classroom, Mrs. Connor called,
"Michael, it's time to go to aftercare." But Michael
stayed in his seat.

Mrs. Connor walked over to him again. "Is something wrong?" she asked.

"I'm not saying prayers anymore," he said.

"Why not?" Mrs. Connor asked.

"Because God doesn't care about me," Michael
said. "If God did care, he would have stopped my dad
from moving far away. Maybe he would have stopped
my parents' divorce too. I must have done something
really bad, and now God is punishing me for it."

Mrs. Connor waited a moment; then she began to
help Michael understand that God wasn't punishing
him. "Mike, your dad chose to move. Now he may have
had good reasons, but no one forced him to move."

"I know," said Michael, quietly.

Mrs. Connor continued. "Let me try to explain. God wants good things for everyone, Michael, but he gives us **free will**—the freedom to make our own choices. Each of us is free to follow God's plan for us, or not. When we don't consider what God or others want, our choices can hurt people, including ourselves."

Learning about free will helped Michael feel better. "I'm still mad at God, though," Michael said.

"It's okay to take your anger to God," Mrs. Connor pointed out. "But it's not okay to shut God out of your life. God shares your hurts, and he wants to help you. Let's think of some ways that you can get God's help with your parents' divorce."

Mrs. Connor and Michael worked together and made a list of ways for Michael to communicate with God and ask for God's help.

The next time Michael got mad at God, instead of shutting God out, he wrote God a note about his anger. Then, Michael folded the note and placed it behind a corner of the picture of Jesus on his bulletin board at home.

A few days later, Michael unfolded the note and read it. He still missed his dad, but the hurt didn't hurt as much. Michael began to understand that God cared about what he had written down, and was helping him.

Talking with God

Michael had a lot to say to God.

What would you like to say to God right now?

Write a note or draw a picture for God below.

How Do You Think of God?

People have different ideas, or images, of what God is like.

Michael thought that God was punishing him like a judge.

Check any pictures below that fit how you think of God (or draw your own picture on the next page).

Then, circle the picture that describes God best for you.

_____ Santa Claus

_____Energy or Force

_____Mother

_____Father

_____Judge

_____Good Shepherd

_____ Superhero

_____Best Friend

_____Long winding path

How Do You Think of God?

In the space below you may draw your own picture or use words to describe how you think of God.

When Bad Things Happen

Like Michael in the story, many kids question whether God still loves them when their parents separate or divorce. That's because it's difficult to understand why a good and loving God would let bad things like divorce happen at all. Suffering is a mystery that is hard to understand. It entered our world as a result of sin. But there is hope because God's grace, the gift of God's life in us, helps us overcome sin. To do the right thing, all we have to do is cooperate with that grace.

Some Things to Remember

- God does not cause bad things to happen, but when they do, God promises to be with us.

- God never stops loving us—no matter what.

- God is the person we need most when parents separate or divorce. Why? Because in order to get through any loss, we need to draw on a strength outside ourselves. This strength can only be found through God's grace.

- God does not want separation and divorce. Instead, God created marriage to be lifelong.

Marriage

is one of the seven
sacraments of the Catholic
Church. A sacrament is a special
sign given to us by Jesus through
which we share in God's love and life.
Since marriage is a sacrament, this
means that Catholics believe marriage
is not only a one-day wedding
celebration, but also a kind of
living in which the couple is
meant to meet Jesus Christ
in a unique way.

Where Is God?

In the story, Michael felt distant from God. Do you think that your parents' separation or divorce is moving you closer or farther away from God?

Draw a stick figure or symbol on the scale below to show how close or far you feel from God.

___|___|___|___|___|___|___|___|___

[DISTANT FROM GOD]   [CLOSE TO GOD]

Write something below that describes this distance or closeness to God. Or, draw a picture about it.

Gaps in Our Relationships

It's important to remember that, no matter how loving and attentive a parent may be, he or she will never be a perfect parent. Perfect parents don't exist because we are all imperfect human beings. Because of those imperfections, we have imperfect relationships with others and may experience that there is something missing in those relationships from time to time.

When kids experience this gap in their relationship with a parent, though, they may throw their disappointment onto God, and conclude incorrectly that God also loves them in an imperfect way. However, that is not true. God is perfect, and his love for us is also perfect. Even more, the Bible tells us that God is love.

Any gaps in our human relationships point us toward God. No matter how much our own parents may fail us, we can trust God to love us and answer our needs.

God, Our Father

The Bible tells us that "God is a father to the fatherless" (Psalm 68:5), and that "if my father and mother forsake me, the LORD will take me up" (Psalm 27:10). While it may be difficult to answer why God allows pain and suffering in our relationship with our human parents, we do know that God will always be there to help us. Through the death and resurrection of Jesus, we have been adopted into God's family and will always be his children.

Mary, Our Mother

Scripture also tells us that Mary is the spiritual mother of us all. When Mary is at the foot of the cross, the Gospel of John tells us that "when Jesus saw his mother and the disciple whom he loved standing beside her, he said to his mother, 'Woman, here is your son.' Then he said to the disciple, 'Here is your mother'" (John 19:26–27). From the cross, Jesus gave his mother, Mary, not only to the disciple John but also to all of us.

All Christians are the spiritual children of Mary. She shares God's deep love for us but expresses that love in a motherly way. We recognize this when we ask Mary to pray for us, "Holy Mary, Mother of God, pray for us sinners, now and at the hour of our death. Amen."

4 Getting God's Help

In the story, Michael found it helpful to write a note to God and place it behind a picture of Jesus.

Write your own note below asking God for help in your life.

If you don't want to ask God for help, write a note to God about what makes you not want to do this.

There are many ways to ask for and receive help from God

Check off the ones below that you will try.

___ Pray and/or talk with God each day

___ Talk with a religion teacher or youth minister about any questions you might have about God or your faith

___ Ask someone you know what helps him or her stay close to God

___ Read the Bible. Choose one phrase or verse and learn more about it

___ Ask someone else to keep you in their prayers

___ Spend a little time with Jesus at Eucharistic Adoration

___ Go to Mass and receive the sacrament of the Eucharist, the Body and Blood of Jesus

___ Receive the sacrament of Reconciliation by confessing your sins to a priest

___ Pray the Rosary

___ Read a book about a saint or some other aspect of our Catholic faith

___ Find God by doing something to serve someone else's needs

___ Other. Please describe:

_____

Offer It Up

Our Catholic faith teaches us that our suffering is never meaningless when we join it with Christ's suffering on the Cross. To offer it up means to offer your suffering to God as a sacrifice. You can do this for a specific prayer intention for yourself or others. Or, you can give your suffering to God to use as God wills. Remember, God made the whole universe from nothing, and he can turn anything—even something that hurts—into something good for us.

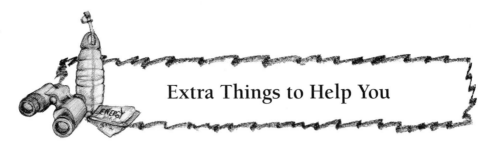

Extra Things to Help You

Think about all the ways that God is caring for you. List these in the space below. For example, consider the food you have to eat, or the persons who love you. If you ever feel distant from God, look back at your list. It will remind you that God is still there for you.

_____

_____

_____

_____

In the space below, write down the names of the people who love you a lot. Next, imagine some-one loving you even more. Write down what that would be like. At the top of this description, write this person's name: God.

_____

_____

_____

_____

If you have trouble thinking of God in a loving way, pray and ask Jesus to help you.

God can help you grow from your parents' separation or divorce, if you allow it. Answer this question: Are you letting this happen? For example, are you blaming others for your problems? Or, are you making good choices and doing what you can to accept your loss? In the space below, write down how you can do a better job of accepting the hurt and allowing God to help you grow.

_____

_____

_____

_____

PRAYER

Lord, it's hard to find hope when bad things happen,
or when life seems unfair. Strengthen my faith.
Help me to remember how much you love me;
that you are always there for me. Give me grace
to accept the losses I am experiencing, and show me
how to offer them up with the sufferings of Jesus.
Use my pain for something good.
For you have the power to bring good from every
situation. Help me to grow from this experience.
Amen.

Take Aways

Write down two or three things in this chapter that you'd like to remember or think will help you the most.

1.

2.

3.

Chapter Nine

Forgiveness

What If I Don't Want to Forgive?

Meg stared at the wall of the small conference room and clenched her hands into fists underneath the table. She knew it was wrong to swear, but she was tired of Lauren bossing her around. It happened every time they played soccer at recess. Even though they were usually on the same team, Lauren, who played goalie, often yelled at Meg for kicking the ball away. *I was just playing defense*, Meg thought, *and now I'm in trouble for it.*

The principal stopped at the doorway. "How's the apology letter coming along?" he asked.

"Good," Meg said. She curled the top of the paper toward her so the principal couldn't see how little she had written.

"If you don't finish it during school," the principal said, "you'll need to finish it at home."

Meg nodded, trying to hide how she really felt inside. She knew Lauren's orders and name calling would only continue, even if she wrote the best apology letter in the world. Besides, Lauren wasn't someone Meg wanted to be friends with anyway.

"Remember to have one of your parents sign it," the principal reminded her, then left.

I only have one parent who can sign it, Meg felt like shouting, *because my parents are divorced and my mom lives four states away! Oh, and since you haven't noticed, my mom never signs any of my papers.*

Meg looked out the window. *It's all so unfair,* she thought. Her mom would know what to do about Lauren, but Meg didn't feel comfortable calling and asking her for advice. *For the past four years, ever since Mom moved away, all she seems to care about is her own life,*

Meg told herself. *If anyone should be writing an apology letter, Mom should be writing one to me.*

The bell rang. The school counselor, Mrs. Santos, stepped in the doorway. "Meg, can we talk?" she asked.

"Sure, Mrs. Santos," Meg said. She didn't want to go to gym class anyway.

They walked down the hallway to the counselor's office and sat down. After a few minutes of talking, Meg shared about her mom and how upset she was that her mom wasn't more involved in her life. She said part of her was angry and wanted to push her mom away, but the other part loved her and wanted to find a way to keep her close.

"That's what we call 'inner conflict,' Meg," said Mrs. Santos. "Some kids solve it by taking out their anger on a classmate because it's safer than expressing anger directly to a parent."

Meg nodded, figuring she was doing just that.

The counselor helped Meg figure out healthy ways to express her anger and disappointment. She also told Meg that forgiveness could help her get rid of her anger.

Meg was confused. "Will I stop feeling angry if I forgive my mom?" Meg asked.

"No, not exactly," Mrs. Santos said. "Forgiveness is a choice we usually need to make not just once, but over and over again," she explained. "And it's normal for anger to pop up even after we've made the decision to forgive someone."

"But my mom shouldn't just get away with this," Meg said. "I'm not getting away with swearing at Lauren."

"Let's switch gears a little bit," Mrs. Santos said. "Tell me what your mom is like."

Meg told Mrs. Santos about her mom's job and what she was good at. When asked about her weaknesses, though, Meg got quiet. She didn't want to admit things like her mom's bad temper and drinking problem. Meg told Mrs. Santos that those things made her feel like her mom might not be able to love her the way other moms love their kids.

Meg started to cry. It felt like she was losing her mom all over again. After a few minutes the hurt decreased, and so did her tears. As soon as Meg looked up, she noticed a small statue of the Virgin Mary on the counselor's bookshelf. She asked if saying a prayer would be okay. The counselor nodded.

Meg asked God to help her mom with her problems. She also asked God to help her understand her mom's weaknesses better. She knew it would be difficult, but she believed that God could help her. She also felt a space growing in her heart, a space that would allow her to forgive her mom. That was the best part.

Forgiving Your Parents

Meg didn't want to forgive her mom at first because it felt like it would be letting her mom get away with something.

Is it easy or difficult for you to forgive your parents?

Explain your answer, or draw a picture about it below.

Feelings that Pop Up

Meg's counselor said that anger can pop up during the forgiveness process.

What feelings pop up for you when trying to forgive your parents?

If you haven't tried to forgive your parents yet, what feelings pop up when you think about doing so?

Write or draw a picture about one of those feelings below.

An Apology Letter for You

Meg felt that her mom owed her an apology letter.

Imagine receiving a letter from one (or both) of your parents apologizing for something to do with their separation or divorce.

Below, write what you'd like this letter to say.

_____

_____

_____

_____

_____

_____

_____

_____

_____

_____

4 Your Parents' Weaknesses

When Meg considered her mom's weaknesses, it helped her stop taking her mom's actions personally. That helped her begin to forgive.

What weaknesses do you think your parents have?

List as many as you can for each of your parents.

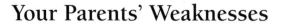

Mom	◎	Dad
_____		_____
_____		_____
_____		_____
_____		_____
_____		_____
_____		_____
_____		_____
_____		_____

Forgiveness is not only challenging to do; it can also be difficult to understand. There are a lot of incorrect ideas about what forgiveness really is. Do you really know what it means to forgive someone? Do you know what forgiveness requires? Not knowing can prevent you from forgiving.

Forgiveness Facts

Fact 1: Forgiving someone can take a long time. It's a decision you often need to make over and over again.

Fact 2: Parents have weaknesses just like you do. Realizing and accepting those weaknesses can make it easier to forgive them.

Fact 3: You may still have crummy feelings even after you decide to forgive a person. It's important to work through those feelings. Otherwise, they can prevent you from forgiving completely.

Fact 4: Forgiving someone is different from reconciling with that person. When you forgive, you don't hold a sin, mistake, or weakness against that person. When you reconcile, you have an ongoing relationship with the person you have forgiven.

Fact 5: Forgiveness doesn't always lead to reconciliation. You may not want to become close with the person who hurt you. (That is how Meg felt about Lauren.) Or, the person who hurt you may not want or be able to have a healthy relationship with you.

Fact 6: When you forgive, you don't really forget. However, this doesn't mean that you should use the hurt as a reason not to forgive.

Fact 7: In order to forgive someone, you may need to set healthy boundaries first. (Turn back to chapter 6 to help you remember how to do this.)

Fact 8: God wants you to be at peace. When you forgive, you give yourself this gift.

Forgiveness Facts

Choose one of the facts above
and write a response to it.

For example, you can share how the fact applies to you, if you agree or disagree with it and why, or any questions you may have about it.

My Response to a Forgiveness Fact

_____

_____

_____

_____

_____

_____

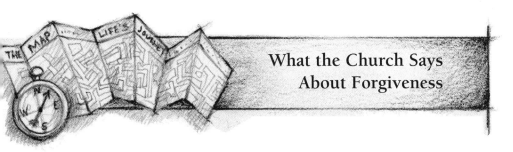

What the Church Says About Forgiveness

Jesus commanded us to forgive "not seven times, but . . . seventy-seven times" (Matthew 18:22). By this, Jesus did not mean that we should forgive only seventy-seven times. Instead, Jesus meant that we should not place any limit on our willingness to forgive. In fact, God calls us to forgive others no matter how much they have hurt us, or even if they don't seem sorry. When we forgive freely we become more like God. He, after all, forgives all of us.

Forgiving others is so important that it influences whether or not we ourselves will be forgiven. The teaching of Jesus states that, "if you forgive others their trespasses, your heavenly Father will also forgive you; but if you do not forgive others, neither will your Father forgive your trespasses" (Matthew 6:14–15). We pray this in the Our Father when we ask God to "forgive us our trespasses *as we forgive* those who trespass against us."

6

A Forgiveness Letter for Your Parent

Read your answers to activities 2 and 4 again.

Then, write a forgiveness letter to the parent who has hurt you the most or the one who upsets you the most.

a) Start your letter by expressing your feelings about your parent and what he or she has done.

b) Next, write the words, "But I forgive you," and continue your letter. Apply your forgiving attitude to your parent and the situation.

_____

_____

_____

_____

_____

_____

_____

_____

_____

_____

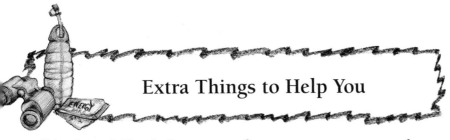

Extra Things to Help You

If it's difficult for you to forgive your parent, ask God to forgive him or her through you. Ask this again and again over the next few months. Then, notice how God, through the work of the Holy Spirit in your heart, helps you become more willing to forgive your parent.

Look back at your answer in activity 2. For at least a week, commit to one activity that helps you work through your feelings in a healthy way. (Return to chapter 2 if you need more help with this.)

Ask an aunt or uncle on your mom's side of the family what they think your mom's weaknesses are. Also, ask an aunt or uncle on your dad's side about his weaknesses. Try to learn as much as you can (empathy builder).

Recognize that you need forgiveness too. Receive the sacrament of Reconciliation by confessing your sins to a priest, and receive absolution, which is God's complete forgiveness of all your sins. Share any difficulties you have about forgiving your parents. Also, be sure to examine your conscience (your ability, given by God, to know right from wrong) by thinking about any unkind words or actions you may have shown toward your parents as a result of not forgiving them. Then confess all your sins.

PRAYER

Lord, I make mistakes, and so do my parents.
I have weaknesses, and so do they. None of us is perfect;
all of us have sinned. Help me to understand my parents
better, and open my heart to forgiving them more fully.
Heal my deepest hurts, Lord, and teach me how to let go.
Bring peace between my parents and me.
I believe that you have the power to bring good
from every situation.
Help me to grow from this experience.
Amen.

Take Aways

Write down two or three things in this chapter that you'd
like to remember or think will help you the most.

1.

2.

3.

Chapter Ten

When a Parent Stays Away

What Do I Do?

"That's the type of fasting I want you to think about right now," Mr. Lopez, the new seminarian at Derek's church, said to the youth ministry group. "What can you give up or change that will help you get along better with others and be a better Christian? How can you do a better job of following Jesus?"

Derek slouched in his chair and moved so the student in front of him blocked his view. Mr. Lopez seemed like a nice man, but Derek wasn't sure Jesus really cared about him. Besides, Derek felt like he had been fasting his whole life in a way, ever since his dad left home nine years ago and stopped all contact with him.

"You might find this hard to believe," Mr. Lopez continued, "but, when I was your age, I sometimes was mean and bossy with kids at school."

The room got really quiet all of a sudden. "You see, I grew up without a father. Never knew where he lived or his phone number. It was tough sometimes, plus really embarrassing, especially since my parents were never even married."

Derek felt like his eyes had just popped out of his head. Mr. Lopez had described Derek's same situation. He always figured there were other people like him, but this was the first time he ever heard anyone talk about it.

One of the students raised her hand. "Did you ever try to search for your dad on the Internet?"

"No," Mr. Lopez said, "my grandmother told me he didn't want that. He's called her a few times over the years. And what he's said is that he's just trying to forget everything that's happened by staying away. That actually helped me when I learned that because I always thought my dad was staying away just because he was a really bad person. I now realize it's not that simple. We all have weaknesses that can encourage us to sin."

"I'm sorry that happened to you," the student said.

"Thank you, that's very kind," Mr. Lopez answered.

I might not hear from my dad again either, Derek thought. He started to feel sad. There was so much

he wanted to find out about his dad. Yet, at the same time, Derek felt a bit more relieved and hopeful because, like Mr. Lopez, Derek had assumed his dad was a really bad person for staying away. *Maybe there's more to the story*, he told himself.

"The reason I wanted to share this story with you," Mr. Lopez added, "is because it shows that suffering is a mystery." He continued to talk, but Derek had trouble paying attention because the word *mystery* kept repeating over and over again in his head. It wasn't until the end of the talk that Derek was able to listen again.

"Remember that our celebration of the suffering and death of Jesus on the cross is not a celebration of

sadness, but one of hope. Something good can come out of any darkness, if we embrace our crosses with courage and hope, like Jesus did. Saint Paul put it this way in his letter to the Romans, "We know that all things work together for good for those who love God."

Maybe my hurts can be used for something good, like Mr. Lopez's were, Derek told himself. He waited until all the students had left the room, then he walked up to Mr. Lopez and said, "Thanks for telling your story. I could relate to it."

"I'm so glad it was helpful," Mr. Lopez said.

"I was just wondering," Derek added, "do you think it's a good idea to get an uncle or coach to help too—you know, sort of like a role model?"

"Sure," Mr. Lopez said, "but what I found the most helpful is leaning on God and remembering his love. Ask God to fill in where your own father may have failed you."

Derek nodded slightly. He thought that was probably a good idea, but found it a little scary. Still, though, he thought he would try. *Maybe if it worked for Mr. Lopez, it might work for me too,* Derek told himself. "Thank you again," Derek said and smiled.

1 Your Absent Parent

There was a lot that Derek wanted to find out about his dad.

What questions do you have about your parent who has left?

_____

_____

_____

_____

_____

_____

There are many complex reasons why one of your parents may have stopped being part of your life. They might even be the same reasons that caused the divorce or separation in the first place. (These reasons were explained in chapter 3. You may want to take another look at them.) Sometimes, the problems that a person has in a relationship with a spouse can affect other relationships in a negative way, including those with his or her child.

Why Does a Parent Leave a Child's Life?

Below are brief explanations of what might cause a parent to leave a child's life.

Put a star beside any reason that might describe your parent.

If you're unsure, put a question mark beside the reason.

Reasons a Parent Might Be Absent

Age

If someone who is immature or has little support becomes a parent, he or she may feel incapable of adequately caring for the child.

Emotional Problems

An absent parent may have emotional problems because of something that happened in the past. If a person does not get adequate help, the problems can influence him or her not to parent a child. Or, a parent may be hurting a lot emotionally from the divorce and handle this by avoiding the child and staying away (as happened with Mr. Lopez's dad).

Financial Problems

A parent may not be financially able to take care of a child. The shame involved in this can be so great that the parent decides to stay away.

Incarceration

If someone is serving time in jail, he or she may be moved to a jail that is far away from the child's home. Often, incarcerated parents have limited ability to cope with life's challenges. Both these factors can make it more difficult for the absent parent to maintain a relationship with his or her child.

Remarriage or a New Girlfriend/Boyfriend

A parent who remarries and doesn't live with his or her biological child might find it easier to connect with the children who do live with him or her. Those children may or may not be the biological children of the new spouse. Unfortunately, it is also possible that a parent's new spouse (or girlfriend/boyfriend) might discourage contact with a child who doesn't live in the home.

Addictions or Substance Abuse

An absent parent may have an addiction or substance abuse problem and not get professional help for it. People in this situation will be unable to care properly for themselves and, therefore, others.

Mental Illness

Usually, a person with a mental illness needs to see a psychologist or psychiatrist routinely and take medication in order to live a healthy and stable life. If this doesn't happen, it can lead to addictions and substance abuse, financial difficulties, or other problems that interfere with the person's relationships.

3 The Good and the Bad

Mr. Lopez initially thought his father was "all bad."

Later, he realized that was untrue and that like everyone else, his dad probably had weaknesses that were encouraging him to sin.

Consider any good and bad memories you might have about your absent parent.

What good points do you think he or she might have?

_____

_____

_____

What weaknesses may be causing him or her to stay out of your life?

_____

_____

_____

If you're unsure, write down any questions you have about this.

_____

_____

_____

God's Love for You

Ever since Derek's dad left home, Derek felt like God didn't care about him.

What are your thoughts or feelings about God?

Have they changed since your parent has been absent?

Write or draw a picture about them below.

What the Church Teaches

When a parent leaves your life, it can cause a lot of pain and suffering. It is difficult to accept suffering. In fact, it may be the hardest thing you ever do. That's why it's very important to remember these two facts:

1. **Jesus knows what your suffering feels like.** When he was dying on the cross, at "About three o'clock, Jesus cried out with a loud voice . . . 'My God, my God, why have you forsaken me?'" (Matthew 27:46). God did not forsake or abandon Jesus. However, because he is both God and human, Jesus experienced what many feel when it seems like God (or a parent) has abandoned them. Jesus knows what you are going through, and he grieves for you.

2. **Jesus is with you.** If you remember what Jesus went through on the cross while you are suffering, you can join your suffering with his, and he will help you through it. You will then be able to find meaning and purpose in your suffering and make use of it for something good.

Can Good Come from Suffering?

Mr. Lopez said that something good can result from suffering, if we embrace it with courage and hope, like Jesus did.
Derek began to believe that too.

a) What do you think? Explain your answer below.

_____

_____

_____

_____

_____

_____

b) If you agree more with Mr. Lopez, explain how this experience may help you grow for the better.

_____

_____

_____

_____

_____

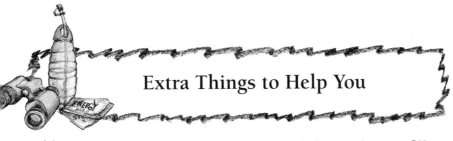

Extra Things to Help You

☀ As Mr. Lopez suggested, ask God the Father to fill
in where your own father may be failing you. Also
ask Mary, the Mother of Jesus, to fill in any gaps
which may have been left by your own mother.
The Our Father and the Memorare prayers are
a good place to start.

Our Father, who art in heaven, hallowed be
thy name; thy kingdom come; thy will be done
on earth as it is in heaven. Give us this day our
daily bread; and forgive us our trespasses as we
forgive those who trespass against us; and lead
us not into temptation, but deliver us from evil.
Amen.

Remember, O most gracious Virgin Mary,
that never was it known that anyone who fled to
your protection, implored your help, or sought
your intercession, was left unaided. Inspired
with this confidence, I fly unto you, O Virgin of
Virgins, my Mother. To you I come; before you
I stand, sinful and sorrowful. O Mother of the
Word Incarnate, despise not my petitions, but in
your mercy hear and answer me. Amen.

Look back at your responses to activities 1 and 2. Find a family member or relative who can help you answer your questions.

Young people often feel a lot of sadness about their absent parent. Set aside a time at least once a week where you can express this sadness and other feelings. Consider doing things like: talking to a counselor, writing out your feelings in a journal, or drawing your feelings in a sketchbook.

When you feel bad about your absent parent, take another look at chapter 2, "Crummy Feelings: What Do You Do with Them?"

Spend time with a relative or adult friend who is the same gender as your absent parent. This person can become a healthy role model for you. Also, consider joining a youth organization or a sports team where you can find healthy role models as well.

PRAYER

Lord, you have promised never to abandon me.
I know you are with me, even if my parent is absent.
Give me the courage I need to carry my cross with hope.
Guide me as I look for answers to the questions I have.
Heavenly Father, I ask you to fill in where my own
father falls short. Blessed Mother Mary, I pray that
you will fill the gaps my own mother has left.
Lord, hear my needs and the needs of my absent parent.
You have the power to bring good from every situation.
Help me to grow from this experience. Amen.

Take Aways

Write down two or three things in this chapter that you'd like to remember or think will help you the most.

1.

2.

3.

Chapter Eleven

Dating, Stepparents, and Stepfamilies

What If I'm Not Ready for Another Change?

Amy walked into the living room and saw her mom taking her parents' wedding picture off the wall. Her mom placed the picture on the end table, then began dusting the wall with a rag.

"Mom," Amy said in an alarmed voice, "what are you doing?"

"Oh," her mom said, sounding surprised. "I didn't hear you come in."

"Why are you taking the wedding picture down?" Amy asked again. Her heart pounded hard against her chest.

"Well, honey," her mom began, "since the divorce will be final this week, I think it's time for it to come down."

"You have no right to take it down!" Amy yelled.

Her mom sat down on the sofa. "I didn't mean to upset you," she said. "Please calm down. Let's talk about it."

"No!" Amy shouted and started crying. She darted out of the room and ran upstairs. Locking the door to her bedroom, she threw herself on her bed, and continued crying. *Mom has no right to turn my life upside down like this,* Amy thought. *Now, she and Matt will probably get married, and Matt's bratty son will live with us too. And there's nothing I can do about it.*

Amy wondered what her dad would think when he found out the picture had come down. She got up from her bed and walked over to the calendar above her desk. A line had been drawn through the current week with the words, "Dad away on business trip," written above it. She crumbled up a tissue and threw it at the calendar. *If Mom gets remarried, Dad probably won't be able to come over anymore and help me with homework,* Amy figured. *There'll be no more movie nights, and he probably won't be able to stay overnight in the guest room anymore either. Maybe he'll get married too and move away to where his girlfriend lives. Nothing will be the same!*

Just then Amy's mom knocked on the door.

"Go away," Amy called out.

"Amy," her mom said, "Open this door right now!"

Amy got up and headed to the door. A punishment was the last thing she wanted on top of everything else. She opened the door. Her mom was holding the wedding picture, but Amy pretended not to notice. She walked back to her bed and flopped down.

Amy's mom closed the door and placed the picture on the floor. "I know this is very hard for you," she said, walking toward Amy. "It's not easy for me either. I didn't marry your father expecting we would get divorced. It's the last thing I wanted."

"Me too," Amy mumbled and turned her back to her mom.

"But, even though we're going through a lot of changes right now," her mom continued, "there are some important things about our family that will never change."

Amy turned slightly toward her mom, curious about what she was going to say next.

"Your dad and I will always love you," her mom said, "so will your sisters. I know you don't see them as much since they went to college, but they do still love you very much. We will continue to live in this house, and your dad will still see you too."

"But," Amy said, sitting up on her bed, "what if you and Matt get married?"

"Even if that happens, your dad still wants to be involved in your life. I want that too. I promise."

Amy let out a sigh of relief.

"Now, I need you to promise me something," her mom said.

"What?" Amy asked, figuring it was probably something she wouldn't want to do.

"You have been very disrespectful to Matt," her mom said. "You make faces and say rude things to him."

Amy looked down at the floor. It was true. She didn't like Matt being around.

"You know," her mom continued, "when a parent starts dating or gets remarried, a lot of kids are afraid

that the new person will take away all their parent's love."

Amy nodded slightly. It was *exactly* how she felt.

"But that can't happen," her mom said. "And sometimes, Amy, parents can do a better job of loving their kids when they have someone special who supports them."

Amy figured that was probably true, although she still didn't want Matt to become part of their family.

"So, I want you to apologize to Matt and promise to treat him with respect."

"Okay," Amy forced out.

"And one more thing," Amy's mom said. "It's okay for you to be upset about these changes. But, next time, let's talk it out. It will help you feel a lot better."

Amy nodded. She already did feel better. "Thanks, Mom," she said. Their family still seemed weird to Amy with all these strangers being added to it. Yet, Amy decided her mom was right. Talking things out helped a lot.

After her mom left, Amy picked up the wedding picture and walked over to the wall by her stereo. She held the picture up and decided it was a good place for it. *After all*, she decided, *Mom and Dad aren't changing. They will always be my parents.*

Family Changes

Amy was upset about the way her family was changing.

She didn't like her mom's boyfriend and was afraid her dad would get remarried and move away.

Some kids feel differently, though, and are happy that their parent is dating or getting remarried.

Below are some family changes that can happen after a divorce or separation. Draw an unhappy or smiley face to show if any changes upset you or make you feel happy.

_____ One or both of my parents is dating

_____ My parent is getting remarried

_____ One of my parents no longer lives with me

_____ My relationship with one or both of my parents has changed

_____ I go back and forth between two houses now

continued

_____ My sibling(s) no longer lives with me

_____ My relationship with my sibling(s) has changed

_____ I feel like I'm the "man" or "woman" of the house now

_____ Getting along with my parent's boy/girlfriend

_____ Getting along with a stepparent

_____ Getting along with a stepsibling(s) or half sibling(s)

_____ Family meals are different now

_____ My chores have changed

_____ My contact with my relatives has changed

_____ I feel like I have to take care of my parent who isn't coping well

_____ Other. Please describe:

_____

_____

_____

_____

A Closer Look at the Changes

Choose one change in activity 1 that you marked with an unhappy face.

Write or draw a picture about this change below.

Family Constants

Amy felt better when she remembered the good things that were staying the same in her family, like still living with her mom and still being able to see her dad.

Check off all the constants below that describe your changed or changing family.

___My parents still love me

___I get to live with one of my parents

___I can still talk or visit with my parent who doesn't live with me anymore

___I still do fun things with my mom or dad like I did before

___I still live with a sibling(s)

___I still see my relatives

___We still do things as a family (like go to Mass, have dinner together, go on vacations, etc.)

___Other. Please describe:

_____

_____

_____

4 A Closer Look at the Constants

Choose one of the constants you checked in activity 3.

Write or draw a picture about it below.

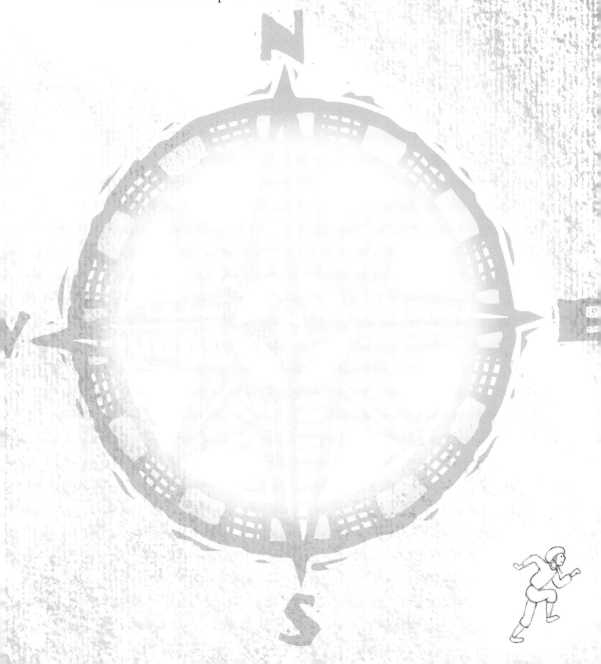

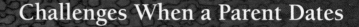

Challenges When a Parent Dates

Many kids feel uneasy when one of their parents begins to date. If your parents start to date other people, it can be upsetting for several reasons. First, dating makes it clear that your parents are probably not going to get back together. In addition, you may still be grieving the losses associated with your parents' breakup and therefore not ready to adjust to yet one more change in your life.

If your parent's dating life is causing you difficulties, you may want to look over chapters 4 and 5 again to help you approach the problems in a constructive way. It's also helpful to remember the following guidelines. Check off any that you particularly need to remember.

___Your parent's dating relationship is different from his or her relationship with you.

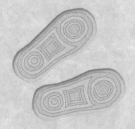

It can be scary to see your parent enjoying time with a dating partner, or begin to develop strong feelings for someone else. If that happens, you may feel like you're losing your parent's love. While a dating parent is giving some time and energy to someone new, this change doesn't mean your parent loves you any less. Your mom's or dad's love for you is unique and separate from their feelings of love for someone else.

____It's best not to meet your parent's date unless and until that relationship becomes a serious one.

It's natural to be curious about whom your parent is dating. You may want to see what the person looks like or what kind of personality he or she has. However, not all dates turn into serious relationships. In fact, it often happens that they do not.

Give your parents the freedom to keep their dating lives separate from their life with you. You may have good intentions in meeting their dates. But don't try to protect your parents from dating someone who might not be good for them. Remember that it is your parent's responsibility to make good choices in this regard, not yours. Giving your parents this freedom may also protect you from experiencing another loss if the relationship doesn't work out. If this guideline causes you difficulty, consider going back to the section on "Healthy Boundaries" on page 112 in chapter 6.

___You've made choices about who your friends are, and your parents will choose whom to date. It's important to respect those choices.

If you meet the person your parent is dating, you may decide you don't like him or her for some reason. Recognize, though, that the reason may have nothing to do with who that person is but, instead, may stem mainly from you not wanting another change in your life.

Your parent is unlikely to date someone who acts rudely or meanly to you. While you still may wish your mom or dad was dating someone different, that choice belongs to your parent and not you. Show your parents and whomever they're dating the same respect that you want them to show you and your friends. This means not doing things like making rude comments, giving ugly looks, or "forgetting" to pass on phone messages.

____It's okay to like and enjoy being with your parent's boyfriend or girlfriend.

It's possible that, after getting to know the person your parent is dating, you find that you actually like him or her or enjoy talking or doing things together. When this happens, it's common for some kids to wonder if they're being disloyal to their other parent, or if that parent might get angry or hurt. The answer is that it's okay to like your mom's boyfriend or your dad's girlfriend. Just as your parent's love for you doesn't lessen if they grow to love (and even marry) someone else, so too your love for your parent will not diminish if you grow to like (and even love) your parent's new partner.

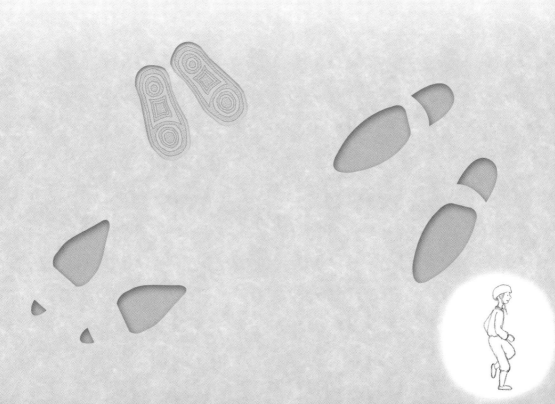

Challenges in Stepfamilies

Adjusting to a stepfamily can be difficult for many reasons. First, you may have more people to get along with. This can make everyday things like discipline and chores confusing for a while. There are also emotional factors. When you become part of a stepfamily, you may struggle with the fact that your prior family no longer exists. That means accepting another big loss, in addition to all the other losses that happen when parents separate or divorce.

If you're having trouble in any of these areas, you may want to go back to an earlier chapter. The following solutions can also help. Check off any that seem worth a try.

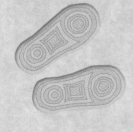

____Be patient. Remember that it can take time for a stepfamily to start feeling like a family.

It often takes two to seven years for people to adjust to being in a stepfamily. So be patient and give your new stepfamily a chance!

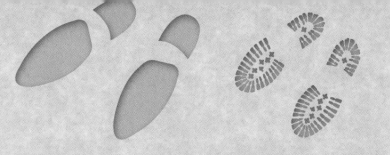

___It usually works best if your original parent initially handles your discipline.

When a parent you know well is in charge of discipline, it gives you and your stepparent a chance to get to know each other better and develop a stronger relationship. Once that happens, your stepparent can also participate in discipline if necessary.

If your stepparent is correcting you and you have hard feelings about it, talk with your parent. Ask if he or she could be the one to discipline you until you become more comfortable with your stepparent. (If you need extra help with how to communicate constructively with your parent about this, take another look at chapters 4 and 5.)

___Blaming a stepparent for problems that don't really involve him or her is unfair.

Are you being fair? Take an honest look at what's upsetting you. You might find that the problem or hurt lays somewhere else. If so, put your attention where it belongs, and you'll heal and grow.

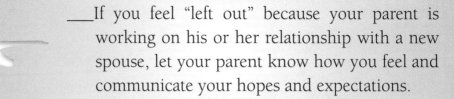

____If you feel "left out" because your parent is working on his or her relationship with a new spouse, let your parent know how you feel and communicate your hopes and expectations.

Remember, your parents can't read your mind! Talk with your parent about this problem, or write your parent a note or email about it. It may also help to make constructive suggestions for how things could change. For example, consider calling or emailing your parent more often, or suggesting that you do some activities with only your parent.

Consider your parent's side in this situation too. Your parent has already had a marriage that didn't work out. That experience of loss may be the reason your parent is trying extra hard to make sure a new marriage works. Your parent may be doing this for your good as well. It is likely that he or she wants you to have a happy and secure family life and doesn't want you to experience another divorce either.

____Suggest holding regular family meetings.

You might feel like you won't be heard, or get as much attention as you once did, if new stepsiblings or half-siblings start living with you. One way to remedy this problem is to have regular family meetings. Remember, a family meeting is a special time set aside when everyone can come together to discuss matters that affect you all. For example, during a stepfamily meeting, you all might discuss which parent will be primarily responsible for disciplining each child in your family or what the other parent's role will be regarding discipline.

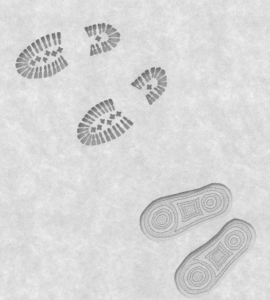

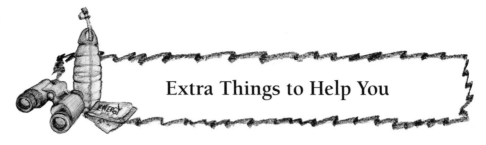

Extra Things to Help You

The family changes that result after parents separate, divorce, or remarry can also be positive. What positive changes have you already experienced in your new family? What positive changes might you experience in the future? (Examples: growing closer with your parents, better relationship with your sibling, added strength and maturity, less fighting between parents, and so on.) Write or draw a picture about one of these positive changes below.

PRAYER

*Lord, bless my parents and my whole family.
Heal me—and them—from the pain that separation
or divorce has caused. Lead each of us to all the good
you have planned for us. Lord, teach me how to love
the way you do, and give me the grace to share
your love with others. Help me be open to even
more change, and willing to give new family
relationships a chance. You have the power to bring
good from every situation. Help me to grow from
this experience. Amen.*

Take Aways

Write down two or three things in this chapter that you'd
like to remember or think will help you the most.

1.

2.

3.

Chapter Twelve

God's Plan for Marriage

Where Can I Find Hope?

"Please open your books to page 93," Mrs. Leone told the class. "Today, we're going to discuss the sacrament of Matrimony."

Kaitlin slowly turned the pages of her book. When she got to page 93, she stared at the picture of the smiling bride and groom. *I don't think I've ever seen Mom and Dad that happy when they were together*, she thought.

"A husband and wife are friends," Mrs. Leone explained, "but they are much more because they have made a vow. With that vow, they promise to love and be true to each other for the rest of their lives. They also commit themselves to the family they may start together."

Kaitlin looked at another picture of a smiling, elderly couple on the same page. *My parents will never be like that,* she thought, *now that they're divorced. I wonder if I'll be able to have a marriage that lasts when Mom and Dad's didn't. How will I know that my marriage won't end in a divorce? Mom and Dad didn't.* She began to feel very sad for her parents and herself. She kept looking down at her book, hoping Mrs. Leone wouldn't notice her lack of attention and call on her.

After a few more minutes, the bell rang.

"We'll continue talking about this sacrament to-morrow," Mrs. Leone said. "Pack up your things and line up for lunch."

The class quickly packed up their belongings and headed to their lockers at the back of the classroom. A couple of Kaitlin's friends started talking about how cute the groom in the picture was. Kaitlin continued sitting in her seat, waiting for them to walk past her. She hadn't told anyone about her parents' divorce and didn't want to say anything that might cause them to find out about it.

"Come on, Kaitlin," Mrs. Leone called out. "We're waiting for you."

Kaitlin looked at Mrs. Leone and nodded, as if nothing was wrong. Then, she packed up her book and notebook and took her place at the end of the line.

The class walked down the hall to the lunchroom. Just as Kaitlin was turning to go in, Mrs. Leone stopped her. "Kaitlin, can I talk to you for a minute?"

"Sure," Kaitlin said and followed her to a bench a short distance away.

After they sat down, Mrs. Leone said, "I noticed you were very quiet in class, not at all like yourself."

Kaitlin looked away.

"I just want you to know," Mrs. Leone continued, "your mom told me about your parents' divorce. I'm very sorry."

Kaitlin nodded and looked down at the ground.

Then Mrs. Leone added, "Your mom also said you told her you don't want to ever get married because you don't want to risk getting divorced."

Kaitlin nodded again. Tears started to roll down her face.

Mrs. Leone put her arm on Kaitlin's shoulder and said, "I can see how difficult this is for you." Kaitlin cried harder. Mrs. Leone waited until Kaitlin had stopped and then said, "I felt the same way when my parents divorced."

Kaitlin looked up at Mrs. Leone.

"I want you to remember something very important," Mrs. Leone said. "God wants us to forgive people who fall short of an ideal, just like he does. But we shouldn't throw away an ideal just because people may

find it difficult to live up to it. God gives us ideals to show us which choices are truly good for us and loving toward others. Yes, you may share some of your parents' strengths and weaknesses, but that doesn't mean you will become exactly like them. You have your own life, and a great future ahead of you. You can make choices that are different from the ones your parents made; I was able to. I have a great marriage and family of my own. You can have that too."

Kaitlin began to feel a bit more hopeful.

"Your parents' divorce can motivate you in a positive way, Kaitlin. Try to learn as much as you can from it, and look to the Church and God to help you. Marriage really can be holy and beautiful."

"Thanks so much, Mrs. Leone," Kaitlin said and smiled. "That helps me a lot."

Feelings About Marriage

In the story, learning about marriage made Kaitlin feel sad and worried.

Mrs. Leone had had similar feelings about marriage after her parents divorced.

Now that you've worked through many of your feelings about your parents' separation or divorce, how do you feel about possibly getting married yourself someday?

Put a check next to the feelings that apply to you.

I feel _____ about marriage.

_____ Excited

_____ Hopeful

_____ Other positive feeling(s).
Please describe:

_____

_____ Uninterested

_____ Afraid

_____ Nervous

_____ Worried

_____ Other negative feeling(s).
Please describe:

_____

God's Plan for Marriage

God created marriage to be a sign of his own love. In order for the love of marriage to reflect God's love, it must be freely given, faithful, fruitful, and forever. That means as husband and wife a man and woman must give themselves freely, totally, and only to each other, they must be open to welcoming children, and they must understand that their commitment is meant to last a lifetime.

Marriage Vows

A man and woman make a commitment to love and honor each other no matter what happens in their life together. Knowing that illness, financial problems, and serious decisions may come their way, they promise to grow in love despite any difficulties they face. Marriage is a serious commitment, a vow or solemn promise before God. Therefore, it's important for the couple to ask God to guide them in making this decision. A couple considering marriage should listen to the advice of the people who know and love them, really think about what they are committing to, and pray about it.

Promises Made to Me

Think of a promise someone made to you.
Was it kept?

If so, explain what you think it took to make that happen.

If not, explain why you think the promise was broken.

_____

_____

_____

_____

_____

_____

Promises I Have Made

Now, think of a promise you have made to someone else.

Did you keep it? If "yes," write down how you kept it.

If not, write down what prevented you from keeping it.

_____

_____

_____

_____

_____

_____

Requirements for Marriage According to God's Plan

It's easy to understand why people should only make promises they are able to keep. Sometimes, though, we may not realize that we are promising more than we are capable of delivering. God's plan for marriage is possible only when a couple—that is, one man and one woman—is capable of true consent. True consent means that each person has made a decision to marry freely, knowingly, and without serious doubts. Neither the man nor the woman should feel pressured to get married, and both should understand the responsibilities involved in marrying their particular spouse. If any of these requirements are missing, there may be an obstacle to forming a marriage in the way God intended. That obstacle can be part of what causes problems in the marriage.

Forming a Marriage According to God's Design

In the story, Mrs. Leone told Kaitlin that we shouldn't throw away an ideal just because there are people who don't live up to it.

What qualities could help you follow God's plan for marriage, if you decide to marry some day?

Write down as many ideas as you can think of.

honesty, maturity,

_____

_____

_____

_____

_____

The Sacrament of Matrimony

Every marriage that is lived according to God's plan is beautiful. But as Catholics, we believe that Jesus raised marriage between two baptized people even higher. Like the other sacraments of the Church, marriage is a special calling Jesus gives to baptized people so that they may grow in holiness and serve him. In the sacrament of Matrimony, God himself pours grace into the love of a husband and wife through the Holy Spirit. This grace helps the couple to love each other completely, the way Christ Jesus loves the Church.

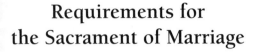

Requirements for the Sacrament of Marriage

The Church teaches that a marriage can only be sacramental when it is formed between two baptized persons—one man and one woman—in the way that God created it to be (free, faithful, fruitful, and forever). A very important part of this formation involves consent, which is the decision that a bride and groom make to enter into marriage on their wedding day. If either or both of them are Catholic, the wedding takes place in a church, usually during a Mass. A priest or deacon must preside over the marriage ceremony, unless the bishop gives special permission for someone else to preside.

Civil Marriage

Just as we live in a faith community in our Church and follow God's rules, we also live in countries, states, and societies that have rules. We call these rules civil laws. Governments have specific laws about marriage. That is why all couples who want to be married—whether they are Catholic or not—must apply to the government for a marriage license. Civil wedding ceremonies are sometimes held in courts or city halls. A Justice of the Peace often presides over a civil marriage ceremony.

It's important to recognize that civil law and God's law are not the same, and that the requirements for civil marriages are not the same as the requirements for marriage as God intended it to be. As a result, not all marriages are formed according to God's plan. Marriage as God designed it meets the requirements of both the civil law and the Church.

Annulment

No one, including the Church, has the power to end a marriage that was formed the way God intended it to be formed. A marriage only ends when one of the spouses dies.

At the same time, though, the Church recognizes that:

- Sometimes, a couple marries without truly understanding the requirements of a marriage according to God's plan.

- A couple may have obstacles that prevent them from having everything that is required to form a marriage that is according to God's plan. Again, this often involves one or both spouses' ability to give their true consent.

When a couple divorces, one or both of the spouses can ask the Church to investigate whether or not something important was missing when the

couple gave their consent on their wedding day. If that is the case, the Church may decide that the couple was not able to fulfill God's plan for marriage. This decision is called an annulment. An annulment is a Church declaration that the couple's commitment never reached the level required for marriage as God intended it to be. That is because not everything needed for a marriage was present at the time of the wedding.

What an Annulment Means for Kids

If your parents get an annulment, the important thing for you to remember is that, before the annulment was declared, everyone—including your parents and the officials of the Church—considered your parents married. Remember that married couples are called to be open to the gift of welcoming children, so your parents did a good thing in welcoming you into their family. An annulment means that in the eyes of the Church your parents are not married to each other. They are, however, still your parents, and are responsible to provide for their kids and be the best parents they can be. Annulments do not affect your custody or living arrangements.

Divorce

A divorce is a civil declaration that a couple's marriage existed for a time, but has come to an end. Unlike an annulment, which looks at how a marriage began, civil divorce only looks at how the marriage ended. Divorce is a legal process in a civil court. It involves lawyers and judges, and may become difficult if the couple can't agree on what their new arrangements will be. The good part of this process, however, is that the judge tries to provide for the practical needs of all the family members, especially those of the children involved. The judge may sometimes use the assistance of a court guardian or counselor to make sure that decisions are made with the best interests of the kids in mind.

What the Church Says About Divorce

While the Church recognizes that at times there can be good reasons for a civil divorce, our Church views divorce as a deep wound to God's plan for marriage and human love and as an event that causes a lot of hurt for all family members.

It is important to understand that the Church teaches that civil divorce does not—and cannot—end a marriage. Divorce only ends the things that result from a marriage, like shared money and property. That is why a divorced person is usually not able to marry someone else in the Church unless there is an annulment of the first marriage.

Divorce and Annulment Quiz

Circle "True" or "False" for each statement below.

a) An annulment is a way of ending a marriage.

True   False

b) A couple must be legally divorced before they can be granted an annulment.

True   False

c) If my parents get an annulment, that means I was born to unmarried parents.

True   False

d) If my mom gets an annulment, that means my dad was at fault (or vice versa).

True   False

e) Legal divorce does not end a Catholic marriage.

True   False

f) If my parents get divorced, they cannot receive Holy Communion.

True   False

g) Because my parents divorced, I am likely to have lifelong problems.

True   False

Check out your knowledge against the answers below. You may even want to share what you've learned with your parents!

a) An annulment is a way of ending a marriage.

FALSE. An annulment does not end, or take away a marriage. Instead, when an annulment is granted, the Church is stating that the couple did not have everything they needed to form a marriage according to God's plan when they made their vows. Therefore a sacramental marriage never actually existed.

b) A couple must be legally divorced before they can be granted an annulment.

TRUE. An annulment will not be granted before a legal divorce is final. This is because, like yourself, the Church's first hope is that a couple can get the support they need to overcome their difficulties and heal their marriage. By the time they are divorced, however, it is not likely that will happen. Also, the Church wants to make sure custody, child support, and other important things which are handled in the civil courts are done first.

c) If my parents get an annulment, that means I was born to unmarried parents.

FALSE. In Church law, when at least one of the parties enters a marriage in good faith, the children of that marriage are always considered to have been born to married parents—even if the marriage is shown to be invalid or flawed later on.

d) If my mom gets an annulment, that means my dad was at fault (or the other way around).

FALSE. An annulment does not decide who is at fault when a marriage ends. Instead, an annulment means your parents' abilities to form a marriage were flawed or incomplete in some way and, therefore, was never a sacramental marriage.

e) Divorce does not end a Catholic marriage.

TRUE. According to the Church, a divorced couple is still married. Therefore, the Church does not recognize a civil divorce as ending the lifelong marriage covenant.

f) If my parents get divorced, they cannot receive Holy Communion.

FALSE. Only *remarriage outside the Catholic Church* would prevent your parents from being able to receive communion, provided that they are not aware of committing any serious sins. This is explained in more detail later in this chapter. See the section "Reasons Why My Parents May Not Be Able to Receive Holy Communion."

g) Because my parents divorced, I am likely to have lifelong problems.

FALSE. While growing up with divorce or separation can increase a child's risk for problems, the majority of kids who experience divorce are able to overcome their difficulties. You can be one of them!

Divorce and Sin

Divorce is always a tragedy, and it is important for us to remember that Jesus is grieving with you and your family about this loss. While divorce is a deep wound to God's plan for marriage, we cannot say that civil divorce itself is sinful. Sins like infidelity or dishonesty can contribute to a divorce, or divorce might be chosen for sinful reasons. But often a civil divorce is the only way to restore peace and protect the well-being of all the family members. Still, any sins either of your parents may have committed are between them and God. You don't need to be their judge. Jesus teaches us to leave judgment of sins to God. But the good thing to remember is that no sin is unforgiveable. God's mercy and forgiveness are greater than even the biggest sin anyone can commit.

What the Church Teaches About Remarriage

A person who has been married, even if he or she is civilly divorced, might not be free to seek a new marriage. God designed marriage to be a lifelong union between one man and one woman. Therefore, a person can be part of only one marriage at a time. If someone's civil marriage has ended the Church does not permit that person to marry until he or she has received an annulment.

Reasons Why My Parents May Not Be Able to Receive Holy Communion

Most of the time, divorced Catholics may continue to receive the Eucharist in Holy Communion. However, if your parent has remarried without being given an annulment first, he or she should not receive Eucharist. This is because of two reasons. First, without an annulment, the person's "old" marriage still exists, and a "new" marriage cannot form. Second, Catholics believe that Jesus made marriage much more than what our society believes it to be. Catholic Christians are called to follow not only the laws of their country, but more importantly, the law of God; this is true whether it is a first marriage or a remarriage.

A Catholic adult who has chosen to remarry outside the Church should continue to attend Mass, but should not receive the Eucharist. A person who has returned to God's law and has received the sacrament of Reconciliation may then be able to receive Holy Communion again. The annulment process may be able to help.

God Has a Plan for You!

In the story, Kaitlin felt more hopeful about the future when Mrs. Leone shared the happiness she had found in her marriage. We find happiness when we discover God's plan for our lives.

Draw or write about something you hope for in the future in the space below.

PRAYER

Lord, show me how to follow your plan for my life.
Teach me to learn from my own mistakes, as well as from the
mistakes others have made. Give me the strength
I need to hold on to what is best, and the courage to keep your
commandments even when it is hard.
But I also ask you to give me the grace to forgive myself
and others when they fall short. Stay with me and guide me,
Lord, for you have the power to bring good from every
situation. Help me to grow from this experience.
Amen.

Take Aways

Write down the two or three things in this chapter that you'd like to remember or think will help you the most.

1.

2.

3.

Words About
Divorce and Separation
You May Hear

A lot of terms are used when parents separate and divorce. Below are definitions of some of them:

Absent parent: The term "absent parent" has different definitions. In this book, it refers to a parent who is completely missing from a child's life and has no ongoing relationship with him or her.

Alimony: Money that one parent pays the other to provide financial support after a divorce.

Annulment: A declaration by the Catholic Church that a marriage according to God's plan never existed because not everything needed was present at the time the couple gave their consent.

Blended family: Married persons and the children from their former marriages join to form a new family, also known as a stepfamily.

Child support: Money that one parent pays to the other parent to help take care of you. Courts in most states usually order child support until a child graduates from high school or turns nineteen, whichever comes first.

Court order: A legal decision made by a court that requires something to be done or not done.

Custody: Describes responsibilities in caring for you. Custody may be given to one parent or shared by both parents. There are two types of custody: 1) Legal—which includes decisions about your health (for example, what doctor you see), education (where you go to school), and welfare (things like what church you go to); and 2) Physical—which refers to how much time you will spend with each parent and when. Courts provide different arrangements for different situations. Here are some of the different kinds of custody.

Bird's nest custody: This is joint physical custody in which children stay in one residence, and each parent moves in and out at different times.

Joint custody: In joint custody both your parents continue to have shared responsibility for your care and shared authority to make decisions about you, even if you live most of the time with one parent. **Joint legal custody** means both your parents share equally in making decisions that affect you (such as what doctor you see and where you go to school). In **joint physical custody** you have substantial time with both your parents.

Sole custody: One parent has primary physical and decision-making responsibility for you and your other parent visits you at scheduled times.

Split custody: Each parent has custody of at least one child.

"Deadbeat" parent: Slang term that refers to a parent who does not financially support his or her child.

Divorce: A legal judgment that ends a civil marriage. Parents agree to sign legal papers that mean the government considers them single again. As Catholics we do not believe this. Our faith teaches us that a civil divorce does not end a marriage that was entered into according to God's plan. After a divorce, the government would allow them to civilly marry again, if they want to, but the Church might need to investigate the previous marriage first (see **annulment**).

Family of origin or original family: The family you were part of at the beginning of your life.

Half brother or half sister: A sibling who has one parent in common with you.

Mediator: A person who helps people, such as divorcing couples, to work out their differences and make agreements so the divorce can be reached without going to trial. This process is called **mediation**.

Non-custodial parent: A parent who does not have physical custody of the child(ren).

Nuclear family: A family related by direct genetic or adoptive relationships.

Separation: An arrangement in which two married people stop living together.

Single-parent family: When children live with one parent who is divorced and has not re-married (or when children live with a parent who was never married or a parent who is widowed and has not remarried).

Stepfamily: See **blended family**.

Stepparent: Someone who marries your mother or
father after the divorce (or after one of them
dies).

Stepsibling (stepbrother or stepsister): A boy
or girl born to your stepparent before they
became your stepparent; a sibling who is not
a child of either of your parents.

Trial separation: A couple's agreement to live
apart for a period of time. A trial separation
can proceed to a divorce, or give a couple
time to work on saving their marriage.

Visitation: Schedule of when and for how long
you will visit each parent after a separation
or divorce.

Additional Resources

There is a wide variety of books available to help children from separated and divorced families. Some suggestions are listed below. As with any book though, it's best to use your judgment and review these books yourself prior to giving them to your child.

Books for Elementary School Aged Children (age 6–12)

Jann Blackstone-Ford, Annie Ford, Steven Ford & Melanie Ford (1998): *My Parents Are Divorced, Too: A Book for Kids by Kids*. Written by children to help others like themselves who are struggling with divorce and readjustment. This book covers subjects kids thought important when they were first dealing with divorce. The goal of this book is to get children talking and parents listening during a time when life seems out of control. Most suited to later elementary-age readers.

Doris Brett (1986): *Annie Stories: A Special Kind of Storytelling*. This book discusses the use and value of stories and provides quality information about children. The parental information on divorce and children that opens the divorce story is a clear, concise, and excellent review of children's reactions to divorce. Tips are given throughout the divorce story to assist parents. This book also has stories dealing with nightmares, going to the hospital, a new baby, relaxation, and more. Also suitable for pre-school age children.

Julia Cole (1997): *My Parents' Divorce (How Do I Feel About)*. Four children give their opinions and advice on issues surrounding divorce. A wide range of topics are covered in a concise, colorful, and pleasant way. Addresses dealing with change, difficult feelings, and ways to feel better. This is an excellent book, particularly for this age range.

Paula Danziger (1982, 2007): *The Divorce Express*. In this humorous novel about a joint custody family, ninth grader Phoebe spends weekdays with her father in the suburbs and commutes back to the city to be with her mother for weekends on a bus called the "Divorce Express," where she has to spend too much time. Just when Phoebe thinks she's getting a handle on her life, more change occurs.

Debra Goldentyer (1998): *Divorce (Preteen Pressures)*. Short narratives provide personal descriptions from parents' and children's perspectives regarding separation, divorce, and remarriage. Discusses typical feelings pre-teens may have when faced with various issues and experiences such as custody, the court system, mediation, and parental dating. Suitable for upper-elementary ages.

Earl A. Grollman (1975): *Talking About Divorce and Separation*. Charcoal drawings and written words help tell a young child that the parents are separating and divorcing, that it is not the child's fault, and that they will be involved in his/her life. Includes parent section that explains the value of each page being read to/with the child. Also features basic advice for parents on responding to the child's behavior.

Emily Menendez-Aponte (1999): *When Mom and Dad Divorce: A Kid's Resource*. With compassionate but realistic guidance, this book reassures children that divorce is not their fault and that they will always be loved and cared for. The author offers tips for working through tricky feelings and working out sticky problems, such as loyalty conflicts and schedule confusion.

Michael S. Prokop (1986): *Kids' Divorce Workbook*. This book provides an in-depth look at emotions and feelings about the divorce. The workbook activities help to increase self-awareness and feeling good about oneself. Addresses issues of anger, disappointment, fear, and talking with a counselor or clergyman. Information about other helpful books included.

Shirley Thomas, PhD & Dorothy Rankin (1998): *Divorced But Still My Parents*. This book helps children with their reactions to divorce. Parents can help by reading the book along with their children. It is organized according to the five stages of grief outlined by Elisabeth Kübler-Ross in her studies about the phases of mourning that follow whenever permanent loss occurs. Each phase is explained in words children can understand. It identifies common problems and worries kids face,along with ideas for coping and feeling better. Includes activities and drawings.

Elizabeth Weitzman (1996): *Let's Talk About Your Parents' Divorce*. Simple, brief book structured around divorce-related topics that are described and illustrated with photographs. Topics covered are separate homes, custody, communication, and parental dating. Multicultural photographs are included.

Books for Children and Adults Living in Stepfamilies

Claire Berman (1990): *What Am I Doing in a Step-Family?* This book contains information to help children understand stepfamily issues. Subjects include how stepfamilies form, what to call a stepparent, discipline, changes in household rules, jealousy, and new siblings. This book takes a candid approach to the sensitive issues involved to help parents and children address the tough problems. Text is most suited to early elementary-age children.

Joseph Cerquone (1994): *You're a Stepparent . . . Now What?* This book shows how to set realistic expectations, establish good relationships with your stepchildren, fairly discipline your stepchildren, parent stepsiblings, and cope with grandparents, holidays, and everyday life.

Marge Heegaard (1993): *When a Parent Marries Again: Children Can Learn to Cope with Family Change*. This interactive children's volume is for children ages 6-12 who may live or are living in a stepfamily.

Margaret Newman (1994): *Stepfamily Realities: How to Overcome Difficulties and Have a Happy Family*. This book addresses the major issues concerning introducing new stepfamily members, addressing the complications of daily family life, visiting stepchildren, including resident stepchildren, and finding time to maintain a loving marital relationship. This is an inviting and comforting guide to confronting the reality of the stepfamily arrangement.

Emily B. Visher, PhD and John S. Visher, MD (1991): *How to Win as a Stepfamily*. The Vishers are founders of the Stepfamily Association of America, and they have been involved in helping stepfamilies for nearly 30 years. The book contains practical information and specific suggestions for adults involved in making stepfamilies work. Frequently, the Vishers use actual examples to illustrate particular ideas.

Movies About Divorce and Stepfamilies for Children

E.T. the Extra-Terrestrial, PG. An extra-terrestrial is accidentally left behind on Earth and is befriended by a young boy who is coping with his parents' divorce, and his brother and sister. As Elliott attempts to help his extra-terrestrial companion contact his home planet so that he might be rescued, the children must elude scientists and government agents determined to apprehend the alien for their own purposes. The result is an adventure greater than any of them could have imagined. The connection between E.T. and Elliott leads each of them to a new appreciation of the power of relationship and the place each calls home.

Fly Away Home, PG. Following the death of her mother, thirteen-year-old Amy is bundled off to the Ontario farm to live with her estranged father, Thomas, an artist/inventor who has shaped his environment to reflect his eclectic interests. One day, Amy's travels through the farm's woods lead to a discovery that touches her: a nest of orphaned goose eggs. She nurtures the eggs until they hatch, and since geese imprint on whoever they see first, Amy becomes Mother Goose. Seeing his daughter's happiness, Thomas does not have the heart to deny her family of goslings. The young geese thrive, but their future becomes less certain when an officious wildlife officer tells Thomas that it is illegal to raise wild geese without clipping their wings. Thomas knows that nature will compel the geese to migrate south, but they've never learned to fly, and with no other geese to show them how, they seem doomed. Inspired by Amy's cause, Thomas decides to use his modest flying skills and hang-glider experience to help his daughter teach the geese to fly. In the process, both Amy and Tom come to terms with their past and each other.

Kramer vs. Kramer, PG. Returning home late from work one night, a career-obsessed Ted Kramer is told by his wife, Joanna, that she is leaving him. After a lifetime of being "somebody's wife," she's going off to find herself, leaving Ted to care for their six-year-old son. Ted, while trying to hold down his job, gets to really know his son as few fathers do: cooking his meals, taking him to the park, understanding every need and fear. For the first time in his life he feels like a fulfilled parent. But then Joanna returns—and she wants her son back. This story is filled with relatable moments, especially for kids who feel caught in the middle.

Mrs. Doubtfire (upper elementary and middle school ages), PG-13. When an irresponsible and child-like dad loses custody of his kids, he disguises himself as a woman and applies for the job of housekeeper for his ex-wife. The alter ego of a sturdy matron works a beneficial change on him as well—but how long can he keep this up? A worthwhile look at adult responsibilities and the pain of missing a parent's presence.

Tender Mercies, PG. The film stars Robert Duvall as Mac Sledge, formerly an icon of country & western music, now down-and-out, and a penniless alcoholic. Rosa Lee (Tess Harper), the young widow who owns the rural Texas motel where he has ended up, allows him to work off his board. As the months pass, the singer develops a bond with Rosa and her young son, experiencing the healing effects of this deeply religious woman's compassion. They become a family when she accepts Mac's offer of marriage, and he continues to re-build his life. He attempts to meet with his daughter, Sue Anne (Ellen Barkin), whom he hasn't seen in years. Despite a nasty dust-up with Dixie (Betty Buckley), his ex-wife, he is finally able to do so. However, the last tragedy he must con-front is one that will truly test his recovery. Less a traditional story than a chain of epiphanies on faith and love.

Unstrung Heroes, PG. Steven Lidz is 12 years old, and his world is fracturing. Overwhelmed by his life with an ailing mother and an emotionally distant father, Steven runs off to live with his two wildly eccentric uncles, Danny and Arthur. Baffled by the tragedies surrounding him, Steven finds solace in the idiosyncrasies of his uncles' strange and wonderful world. It is there that he begins the journey from boyhood innocence to a young man's understanding of life.

Acknowledgments

First and foremost, I would like to thank God for giving me the ability, strength, and fortitude it took to complete this book. When I found myself resisting this work because it seemed too difficult or too painful, God was the one who gave me the insight and grace to persevere.

I want to thank Pauline Books and Media for giving me the opportunity to write this book and the creative freedom to write it the way I felt was best. I would also like to thank my editor, Jaymie Stuart Wolfe, who not only provided exceptional editorial talent and expertise, but who also set very high standards which encouraged me to do my best work.

In addition, I am profoundly grateful to all those in the Catholic Church who have supported me in this ministry. A special thanks goes out to His Eminence Donald Cardinal W. Wuerl who was supportive of my work from the start. I also thank His Eminence Francis Cardinal George, O.M.I. and my other endorsers for their generous consideration. We are all blessed and enriched by their service on behalf of our Church.

Finally, I want to thank my parents, Robert and Dolores. Dad, you instilled in me a love of writing, a desire to achieve, and a passion to try and make a difference in this world. Your example motivates me more than you will ever know. Mom, your high expectations have nurtured me to do my best in all areas of my life. You have shown me what it means to be kind and loving towards others. That example, and your unwavering devotion, have inspired my dedication to the young people I serve.

Thank you both for raising me in our beautiful Catholic faith.

Lynn Cassella-Kapusinski, MS, NCC,
knows the difficulties faced by children of
divorce families because she has lived
through them herself. Equipped with a BA
from the University of Notre Dame and
a MS in Pastoral Counseling from Loyola
University Maryland, Lynn is a National
Certified Counselor and a Catholic school
counselor. Her professional experience
includes conducting family, individual, and
group therapy with children, teens, young
adults, and adults. Through her Faith
Journeys Foundation, Lynn ministers to
children struggling with their parents'
separation or divorce.

Pauline
BOOKS & MEDIA

The Daughters of St. Paul operate book and media centers at the following addresses. Visit, call or write the one nearest you today, or find us at www.pauline.org

CALIFORNIA
3908 Sepulveda Blvd, Culver City, CA 90230   310-397-8676
935 Brewster Avenue, Redwood City, CA 94063   650-369-4230
5945 Balboa Avenue, San Diego, CA 92111   858-565-9181

FLORIDA
145 S.W. 107th Avenue, Miami, FL 33174   305-559-6715

HAWAII
1143 Bishop Street, Honolulu, HI 96813   808-521-2731
Neighbor Islands call: 866-521-2731

ILLINOIS
172 North Michigan Avenue, Chicago, IL 60601   312-346-4228

LOUISIANA
4403 Veterans Memorial Blvd, Metairie, LA 70006   504-887-7631

MASSACHUSETTS
885 Providence Hwy, Dedham, MA 02026   781-326-5385

MISSOURI
9804 Watson Road, St. Louis, MO 63126   314-965-3512

NEW YORK
64 West 38th Street, New York, NY 10018   212-754-1110

PENNSYLVANIA
Philadelphia—relocating   215-676-9494

SOUTH CAROLINA
243 King Street, Charleston, SC 29401   843-577-0175

VIRGINIA
1025 King Street, Alexandria, VA 22314   703-549-3806

CANADA
3022 Dufferin Street, Toronto, ON M6B 3T5   416-781-9131